THE NEBBISH PRINCIPLE

A CARTOON COMMENTARY BY ALLEN UNGER

DEVORA
PUBLISHING

THE NEBBISH PRINCIPLE

Published by Devora Publishing Company

Text and Illustrations Copyright © 2002 by Allen Unger

Cover Design: Benjie Herskowitz

Cloth ISBN: 1-930143-35-4
Paper ISBN: 1-930143-36-2

Devora Publishing Company
        40 East 78th Street, Suite 16D
        New York, New York 10021
        Tel: (800) 232-2931
        Fax: (212) 472-6253
Email: pop@netvision.net.il
Web Site: www.pitspopany.com

Printed in Hong Kong

Foreword

Webster's dictionary defines nebbish as "a poor, unfortunate, or ineffectual person." And who would argue with Webster? But in the Yiddish language, a nebbish describes a person whose life is dictated by the simple proposition: "If it can go wrong it will go wrong – and it will happen to me."

The ability to make a nebbish of ourselves is given to all of us. Some exist with this condition on a permanent basis; others can just turn it on at will, such as Charlie Chaplin or Jerry Lewis.

Of course, being on the fortunate, effectual side of the nebbish equation is always preferable to being on the "wrong" side of nebbishness. But I daresay that all of us have, at one time or another, felt the discomfort and humiliation of acting like a nebbish, wishing that the earth would open up and swallow us, whole.

Unlike you, gentle reader, the characters in this book are professional nebbishes – life's perennial losers – and seem to attract bad luck in waves. They come in both sexes(although single males seem to be more common than single females), old or young (unlike the old, the young do occasionally grow out of it), rich or poor (usually poor, because if you're rich, Webster's definition doesn't hold), and smart or dumb (although a really dumb nebbish is more of a schlemiel – see Webster's – than a nebbish).

If you know a professional nebbish, be sensitive to the fact that he or she may not even know they have this condition, and it certainly will not help to point it out. Nor do you need to worry about "catching" the nebbish condition. It's disastrous affects cannot be transferred by physical contact nor by any airborne mode, although "nebbish by association" is something you should watch out for.

All of the characters in this book are fictitious. Any resemblance to anybody living or dead is entirely coincidental, but, incidentally, if you recognize yourself within these pages, don't feel bad - as one nebbish to another, isn't it nice to know that you're not alone?

This book is dedicated
to my wife
Lillian
who is usually right
in the end.

Allen Unger

Allen first discovered that he could draw well enough for people to notice, at around the age of five, although Sioux Indians and Roman soldiers featured obsessively in the same drawings. With such people in short supply as models in London's East End (where Allen grew up), he began to utilize local models who became the source upon which he built his acknowledged expertise in the growing field of Nebbish portraits.

Completing a five year course as an apprentice compositor, while at the same time, studying graphic design at art college, Allen's world took a 180 degree turn, counter-clockwise, when he was drafted into the British Army as number 23787223 (this is now his lucky number). When he was set free, Allen taught typography at The Hornsey College of Art. He then entered the irresistible field of business, where for 25 years as 'Invitations North-West' he used his considerable talents in graphic art and illustration to create top-of-the-range wedding and bar/bat mitzvah invitation cards for North-West London Jewish society.

Allen remains disappointed to this day that, during his quarter century in business, having successfully conquered every invitation hurdle, not one Sioux Indian or Roman soldier saw fit to trust Invitations N–W with invitation cards for their simcha.

In 1995, Allen and his wife Lillian emigrated to Israel, where he discovered a hitherto unknown species of nebbish which will be the subject of his next book.

"Mrs. Goldman, I have completed my examination of your late husband's finances, and I have to say that his death was a shrewd business move."

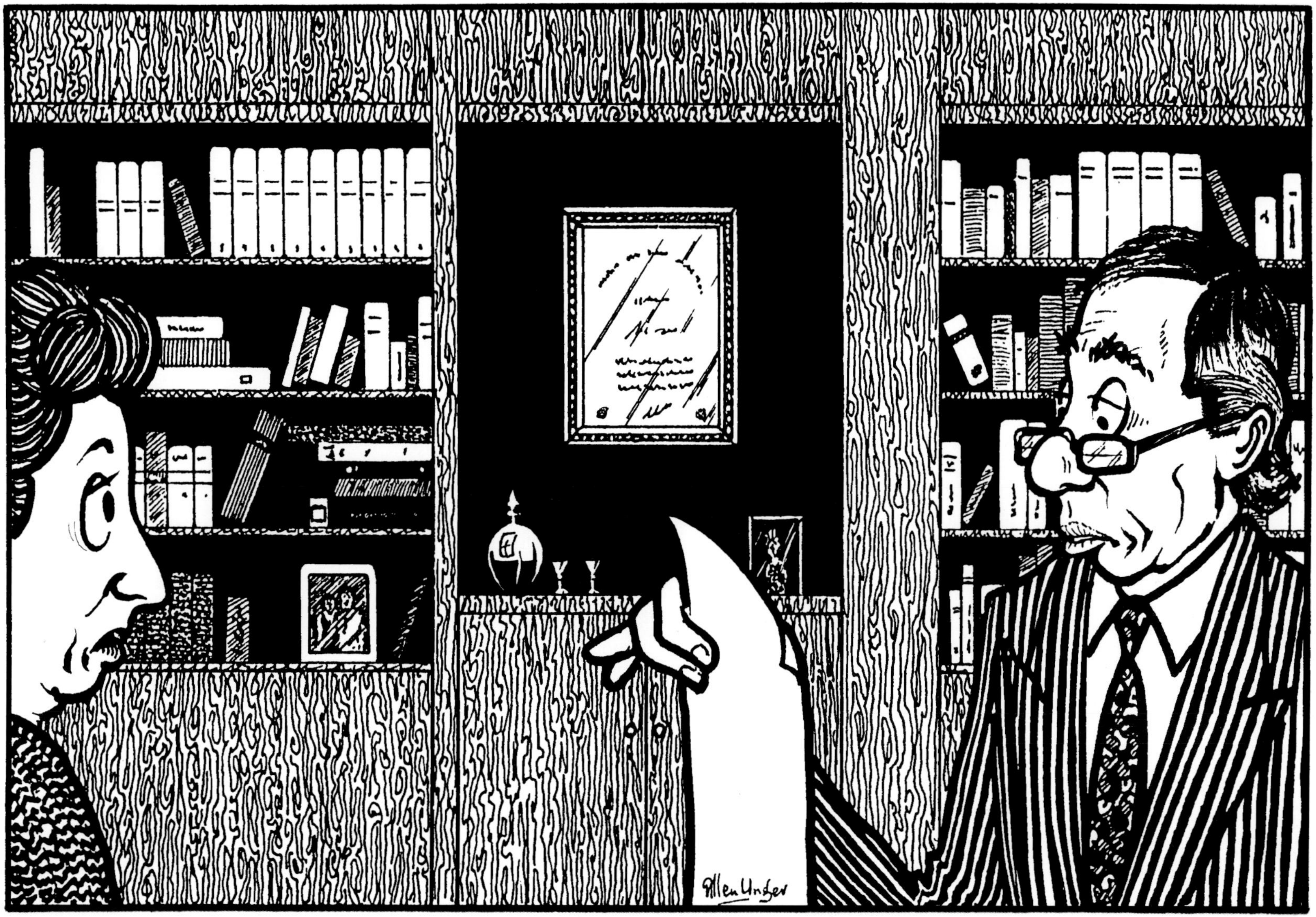
Allen Unger

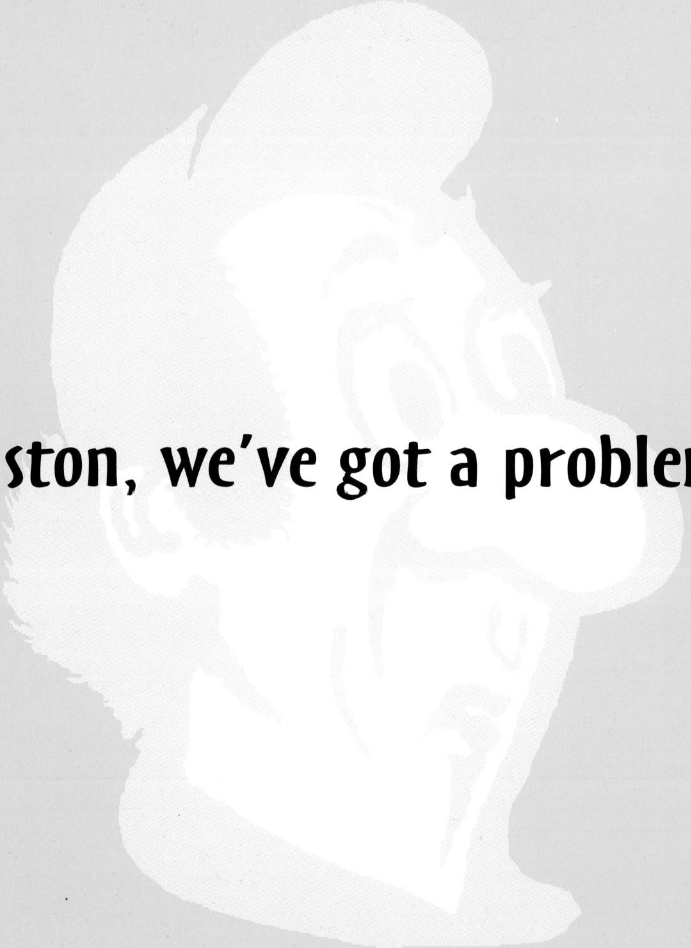

"Houston, we've got a problem..."

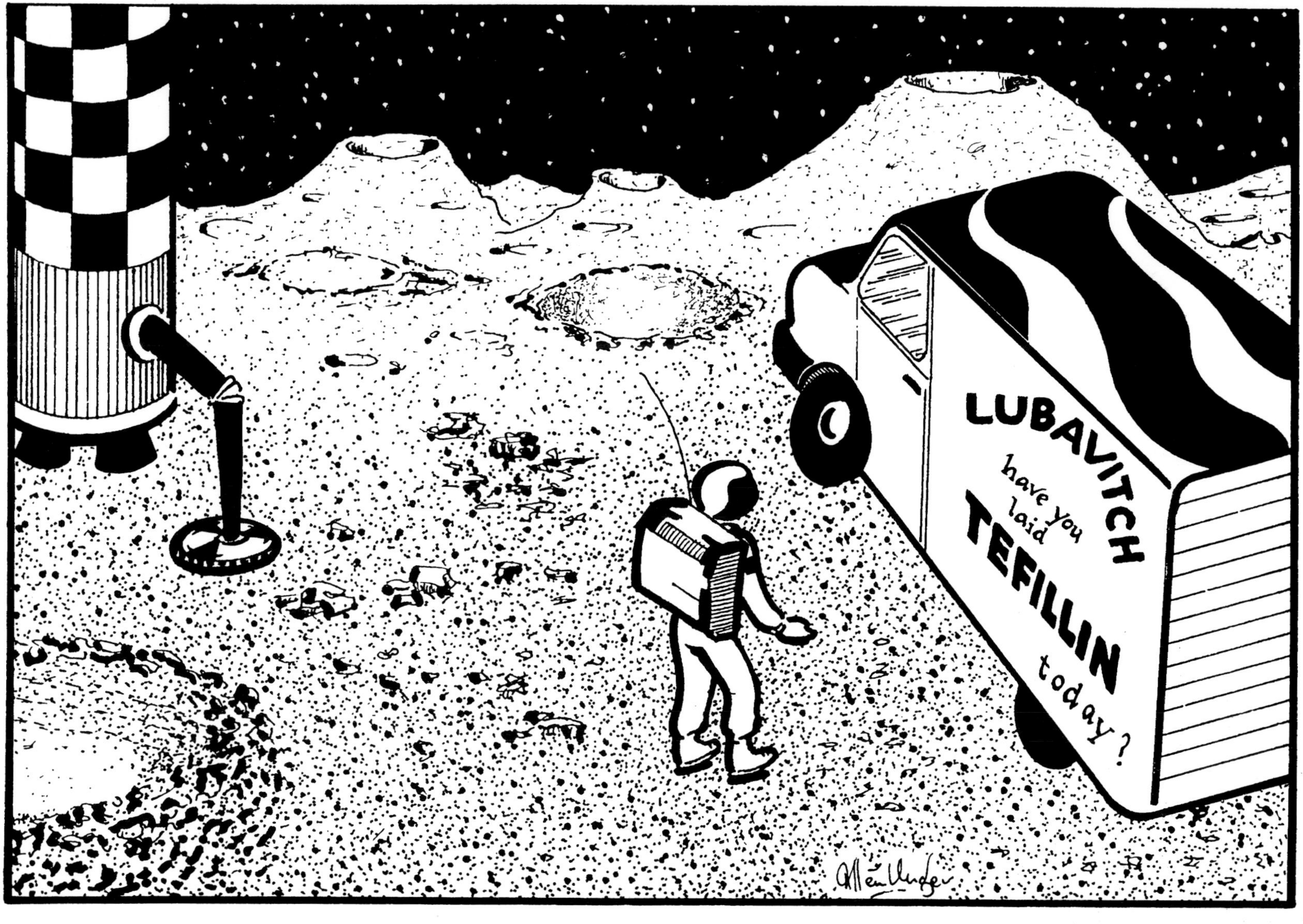
LUBAVITCH
have you laid
TEFILLIN
today?

"If you've got any sense, you'll get that farschtunkaner tank out of the way, or else I'll come up there. Big as you are, I was in WWII boy!"

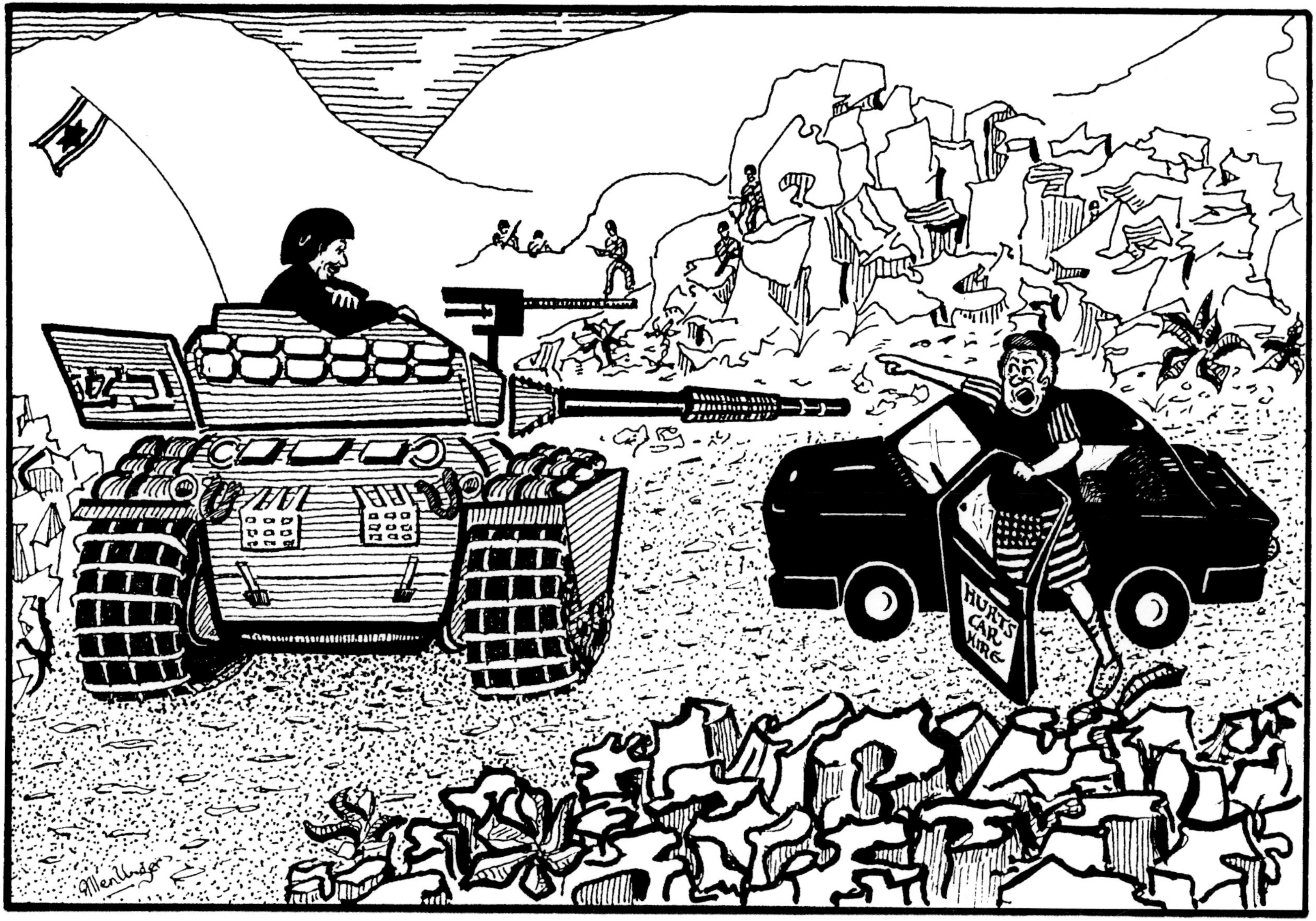
HURTS CAR HIRE

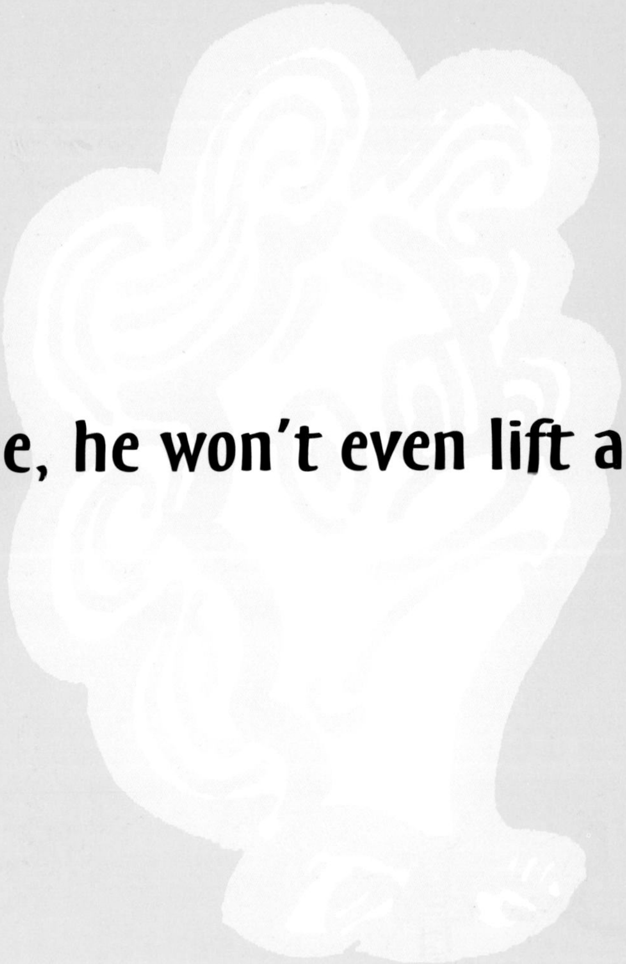

"At home, he won't even lift a finger."

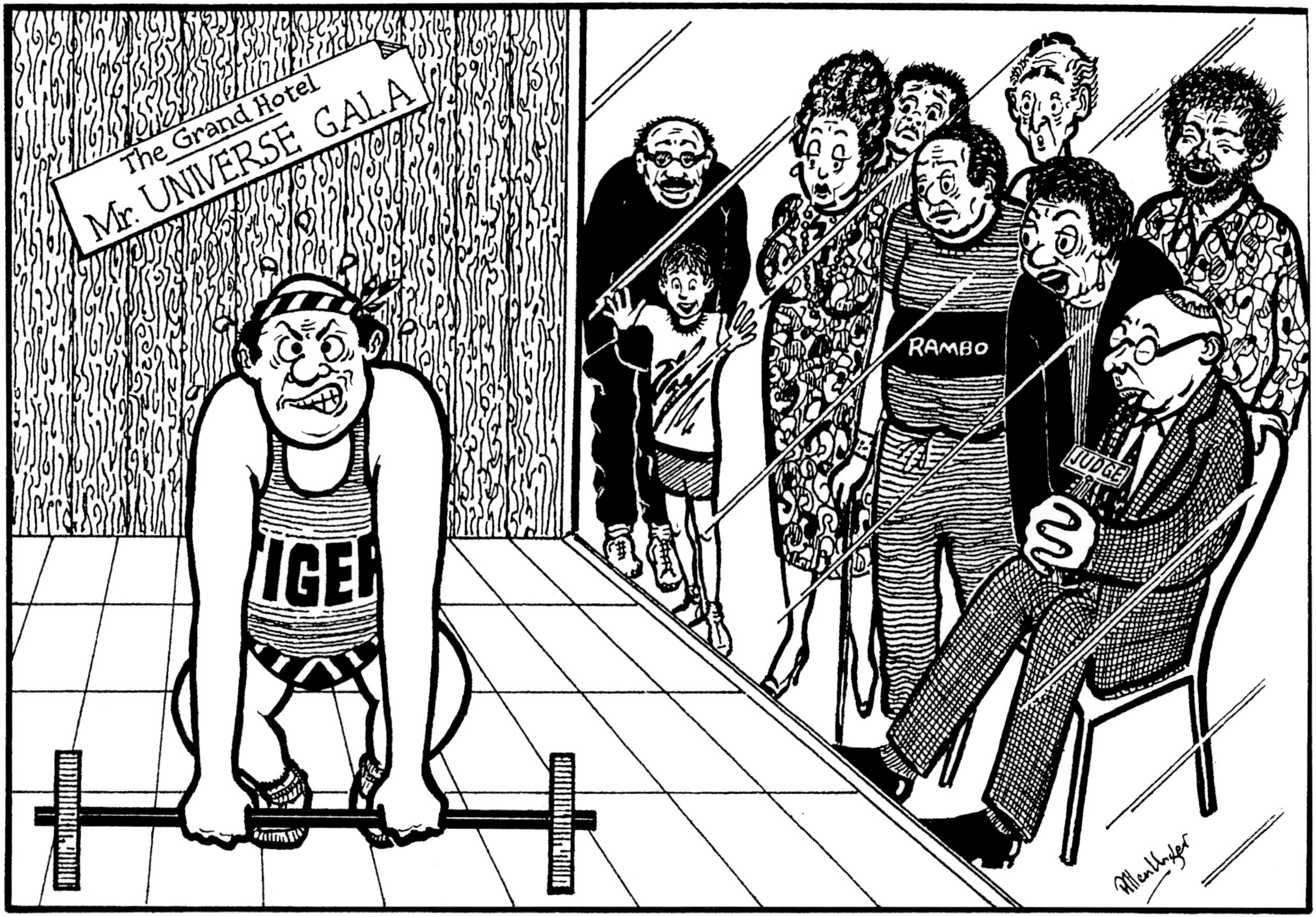
The Grand Hotel
Mr. UNIVERSE GALA
TIGER
RAMBO
JUDGE

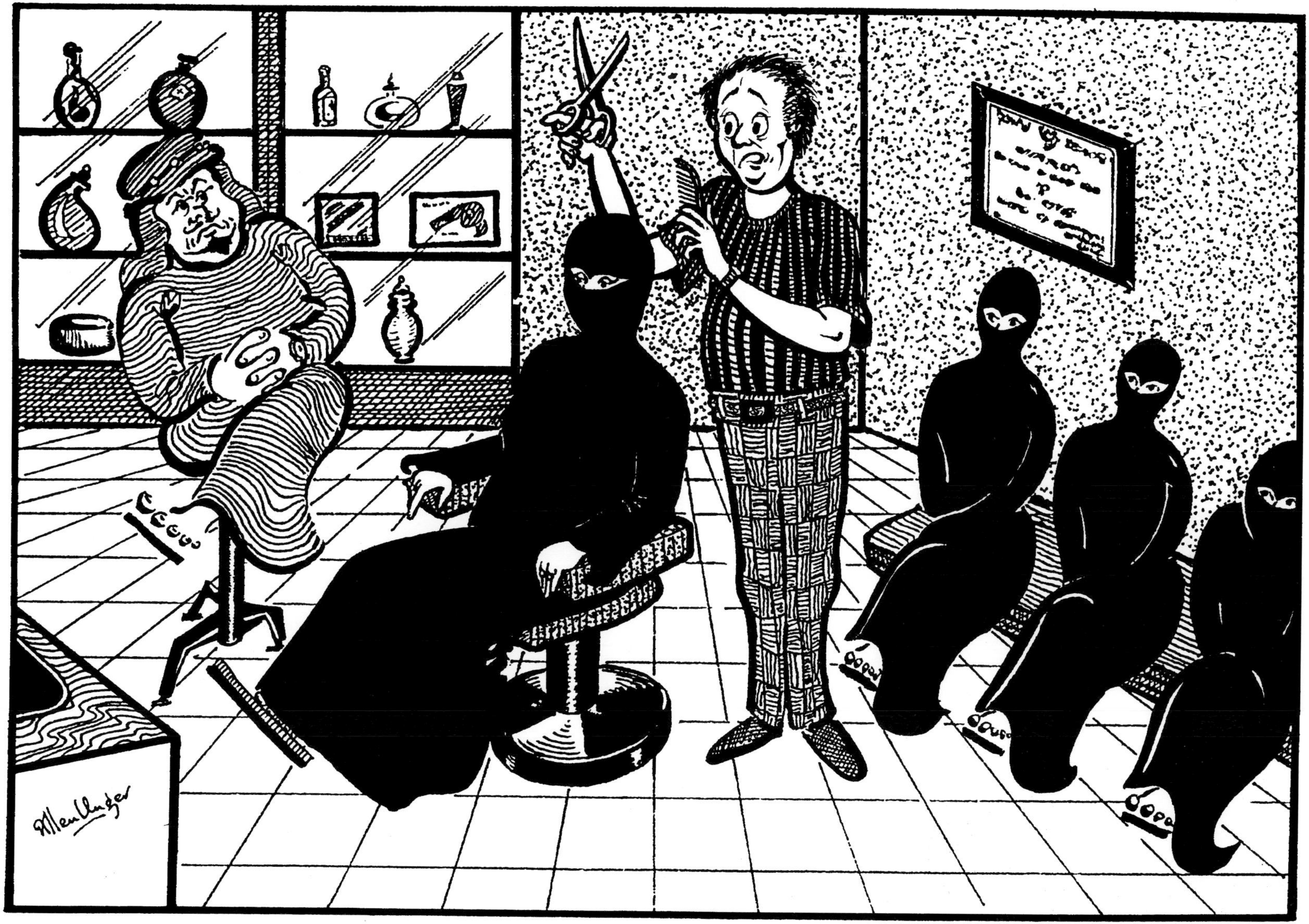

"He says that he's from the Lost Tribes of Israel, and that he's the first of 750 million just like him, and that they're all coming home!"

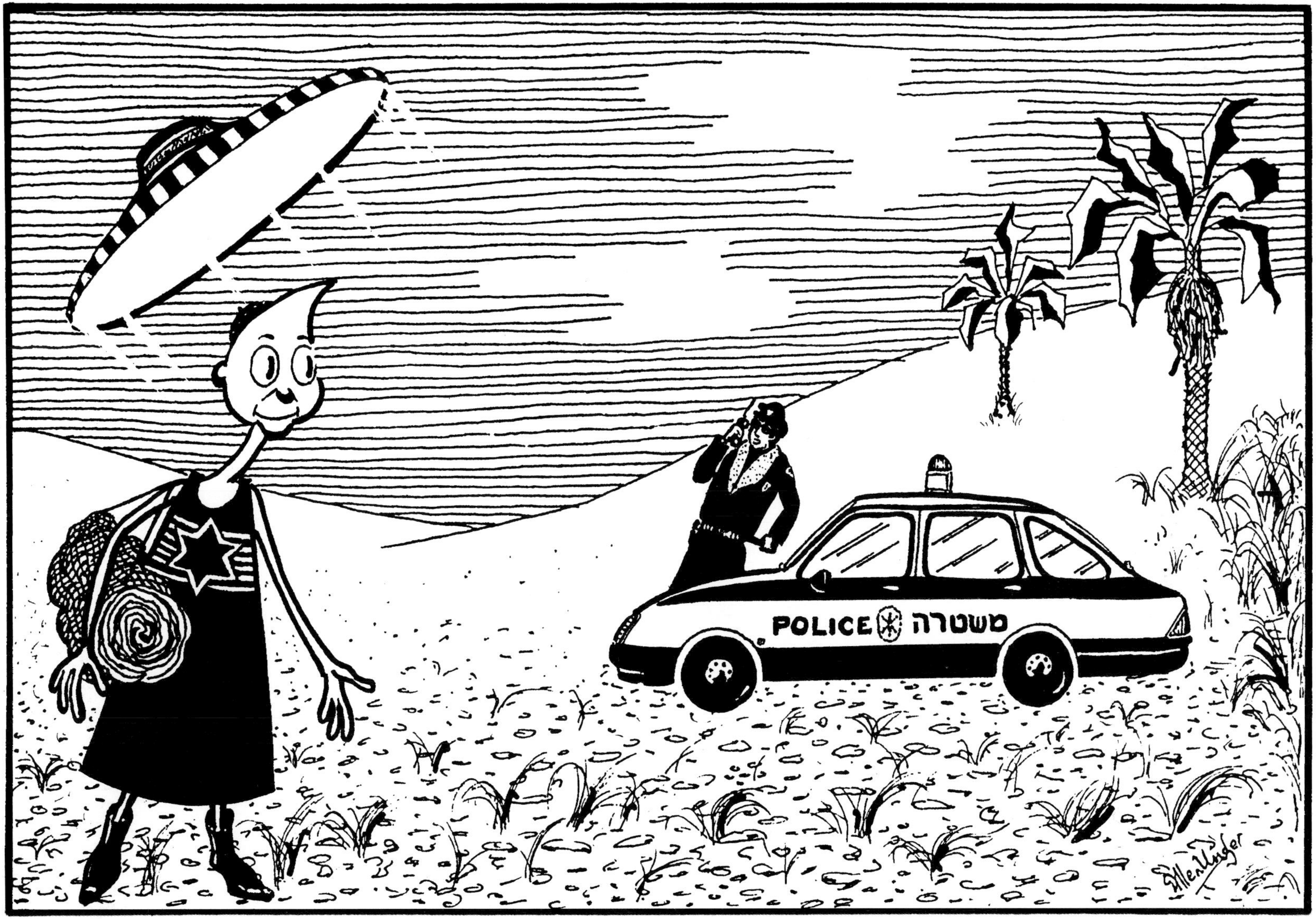
POLICE
משטרה

"Hey guys, remember how I would tell Sid the shnorrer that you can't take it with you; well he's coming up, and guess what...?"

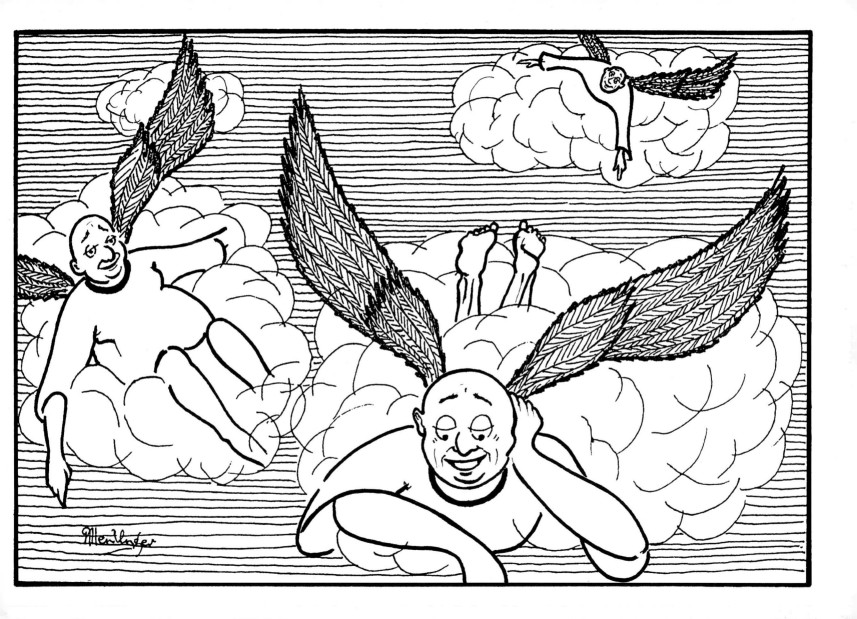

The Battle of the Bubbas

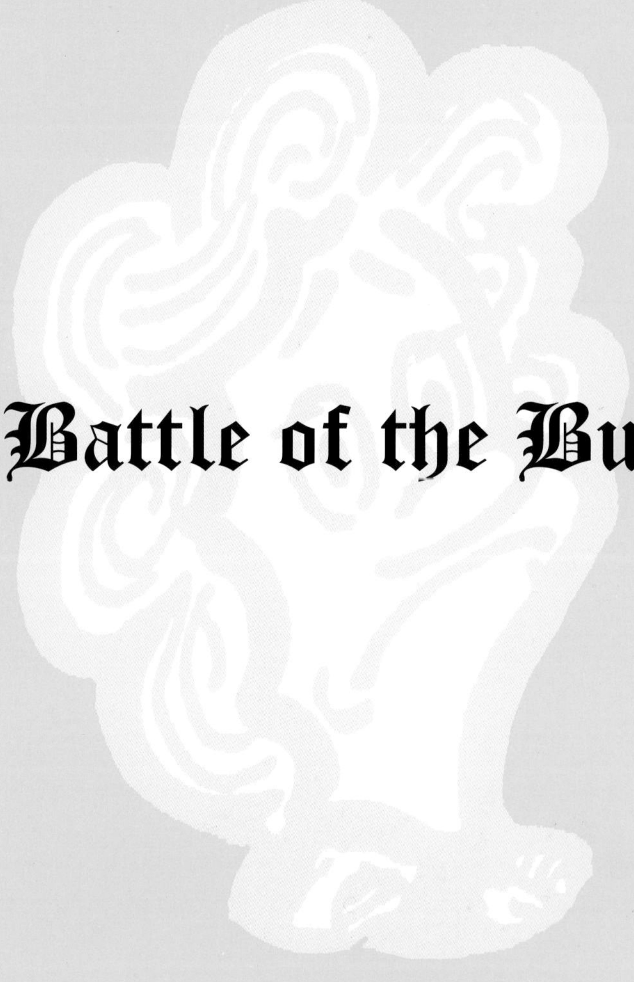

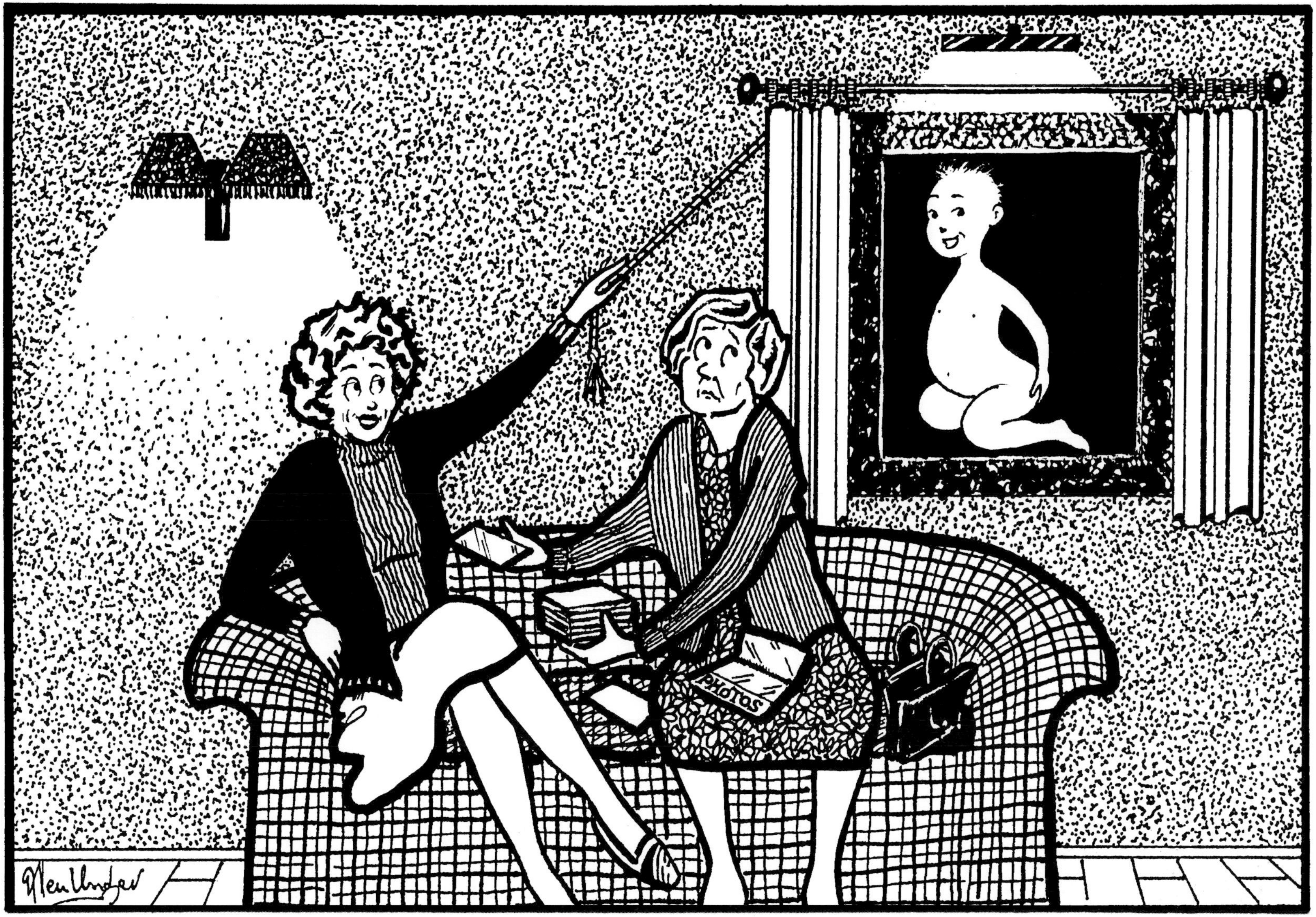
PHOTOS

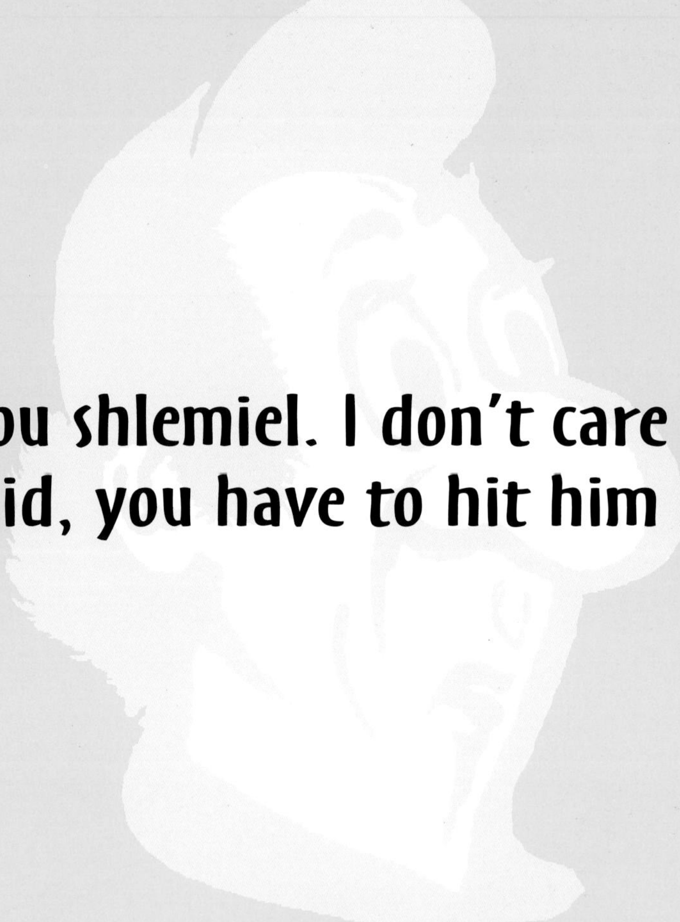

"Get up you shlemiel. I don't care what your mother said, you have to hit him back!"

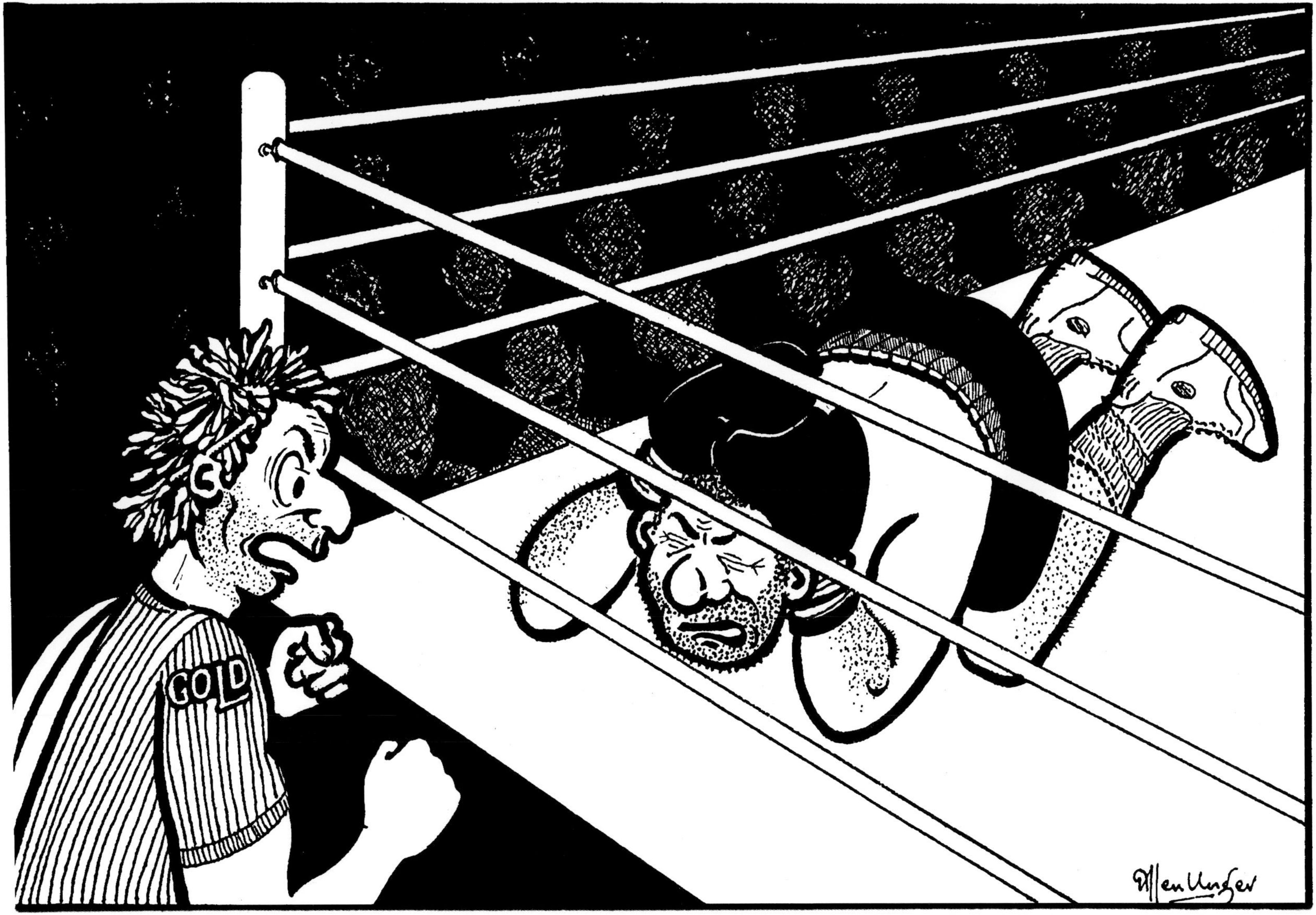
GOLD

"♪ Suddenly, I'm not half the man I used to be ♪♪"

"From where I'm sitting Henry, you're 3½ times the man you used to be."

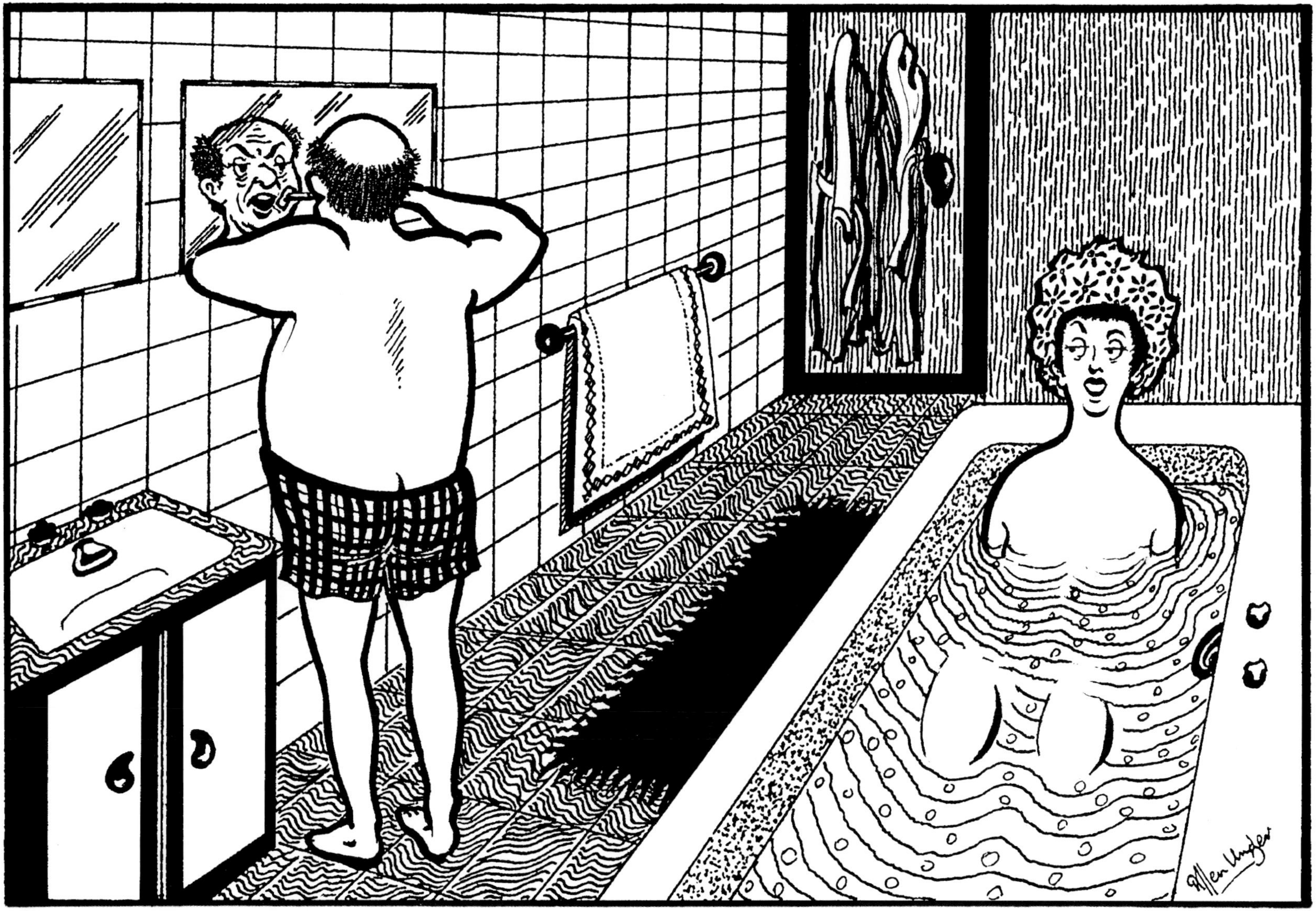

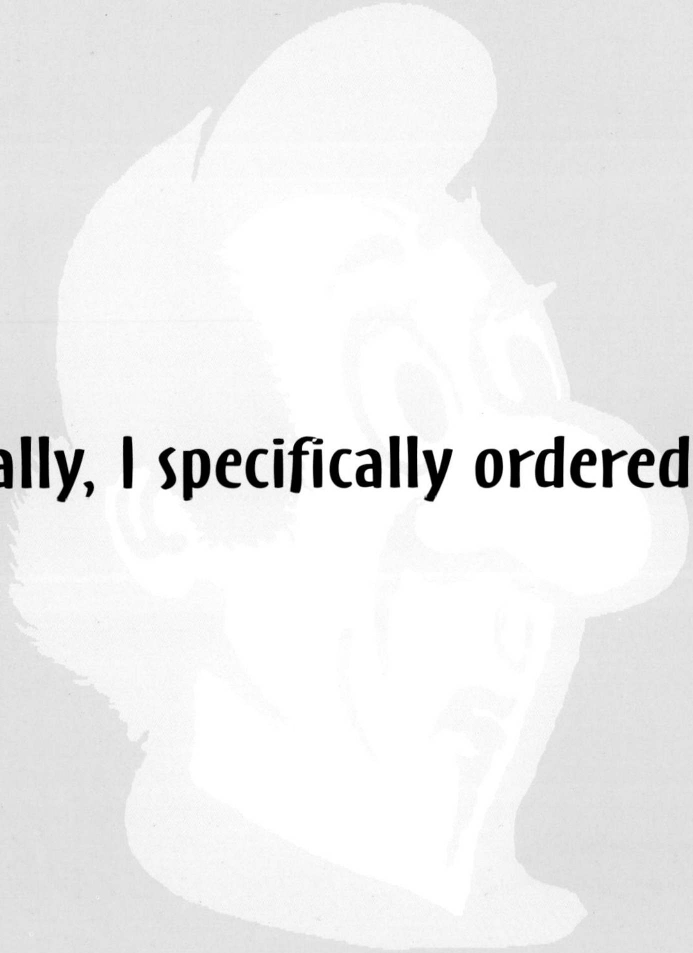

"Umm...Actually, I specifically ordered Non-Kosher."

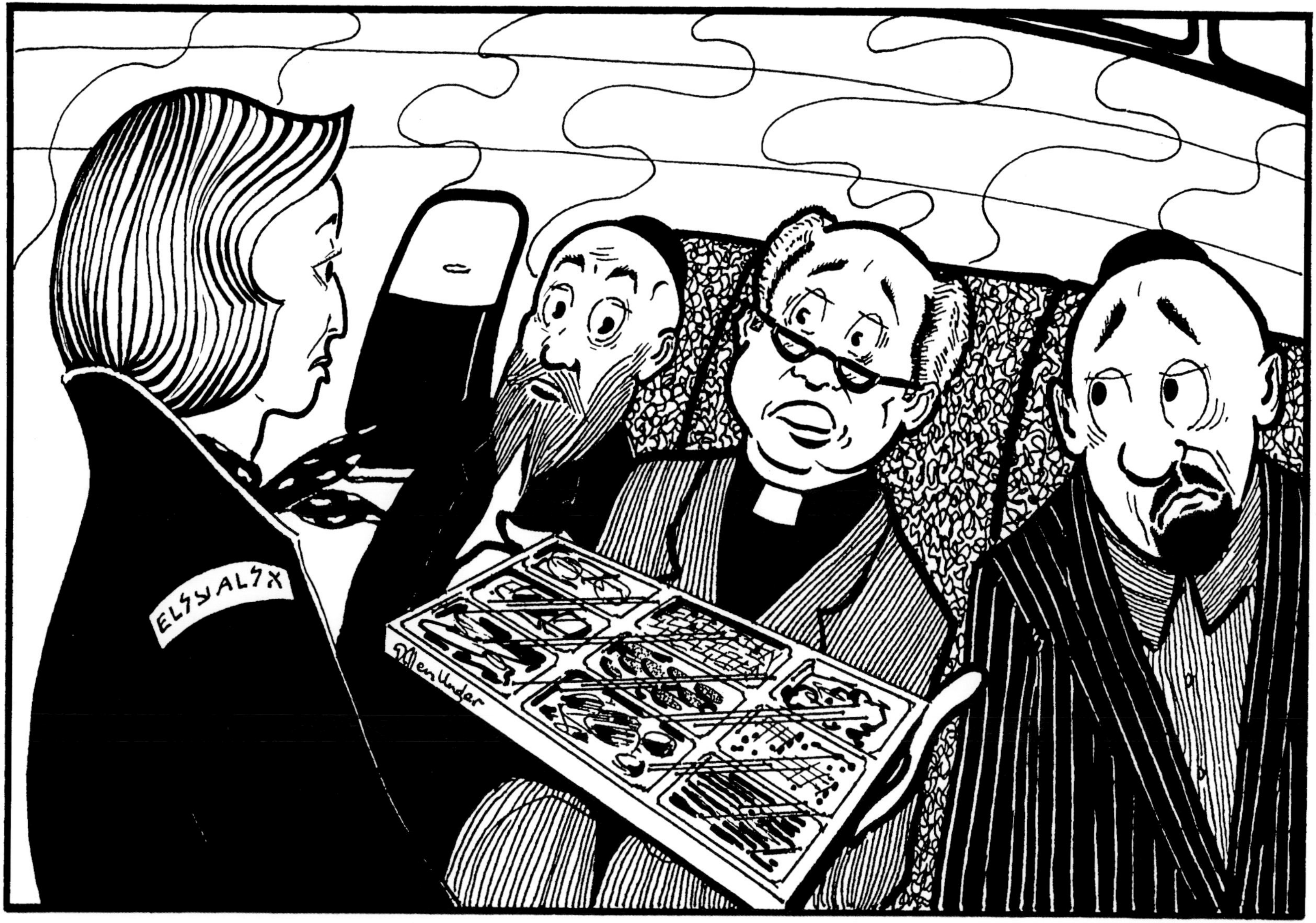

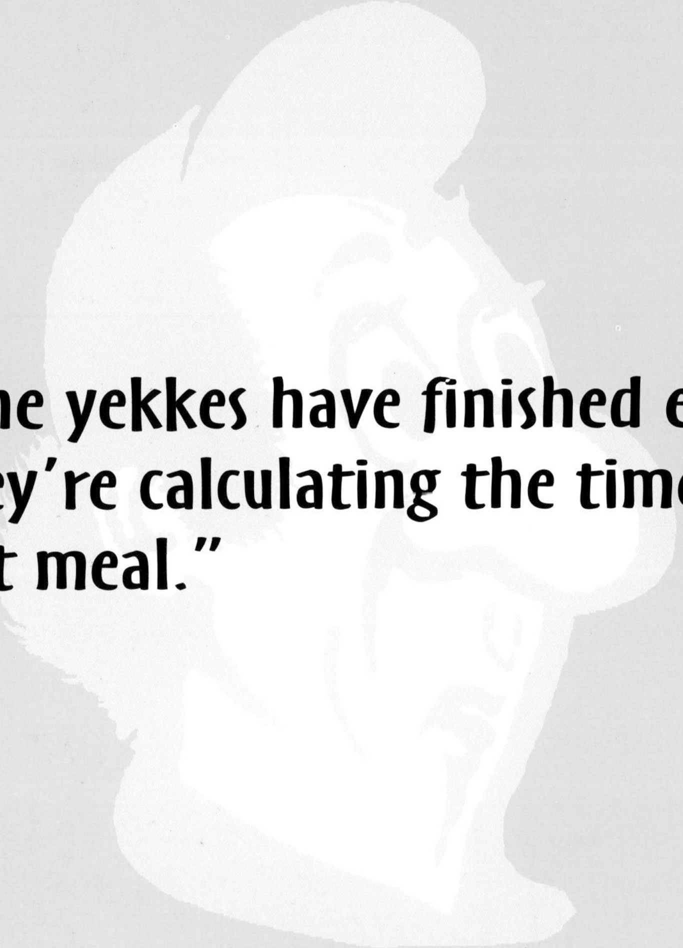

"I see the yekkes have finished eating... Now they're calculating the time before the next meal."

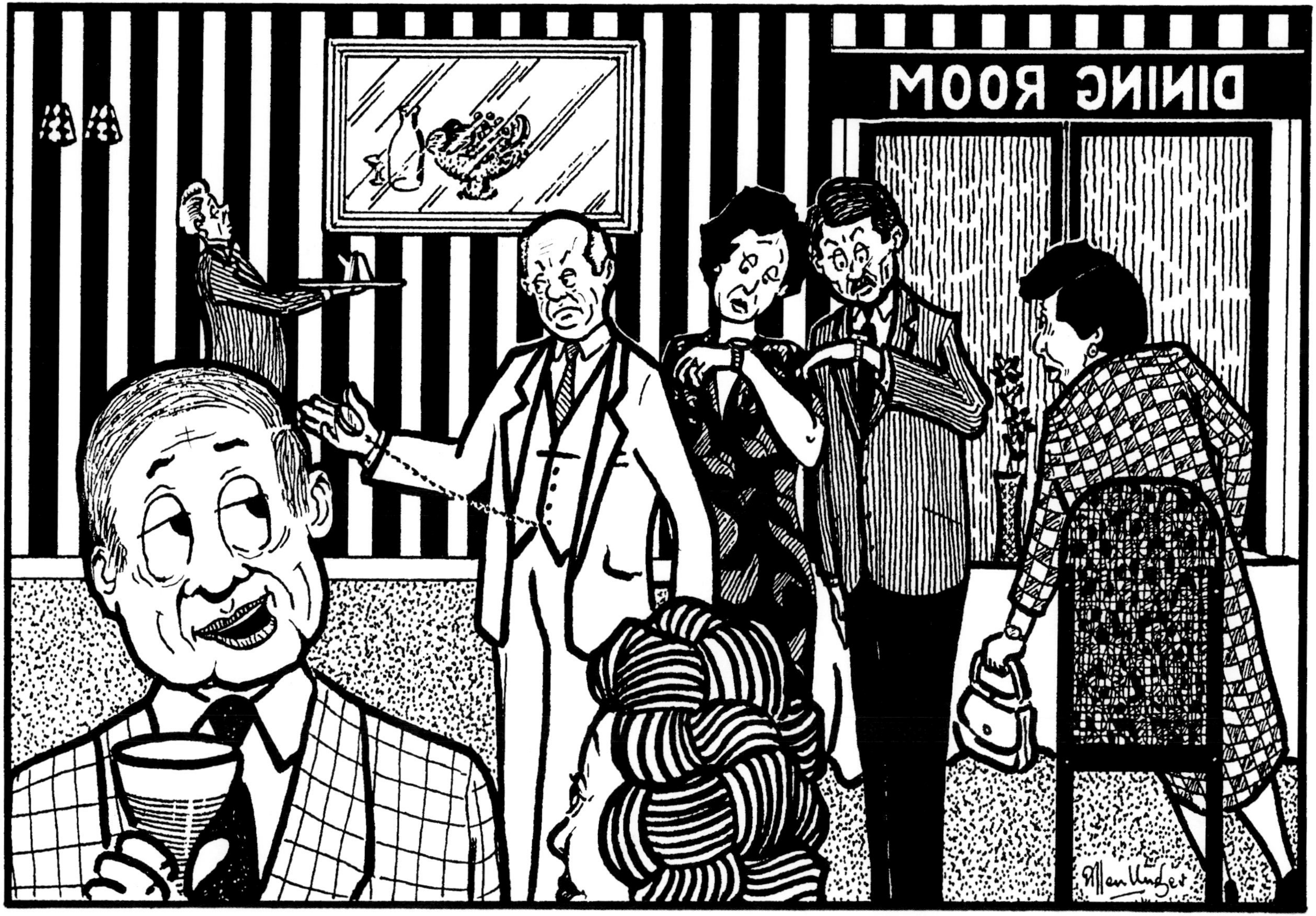
DINING ROOM
Allen Unger

"They could be dancing the tango, but it's more likely that their backs are verkrimmt."

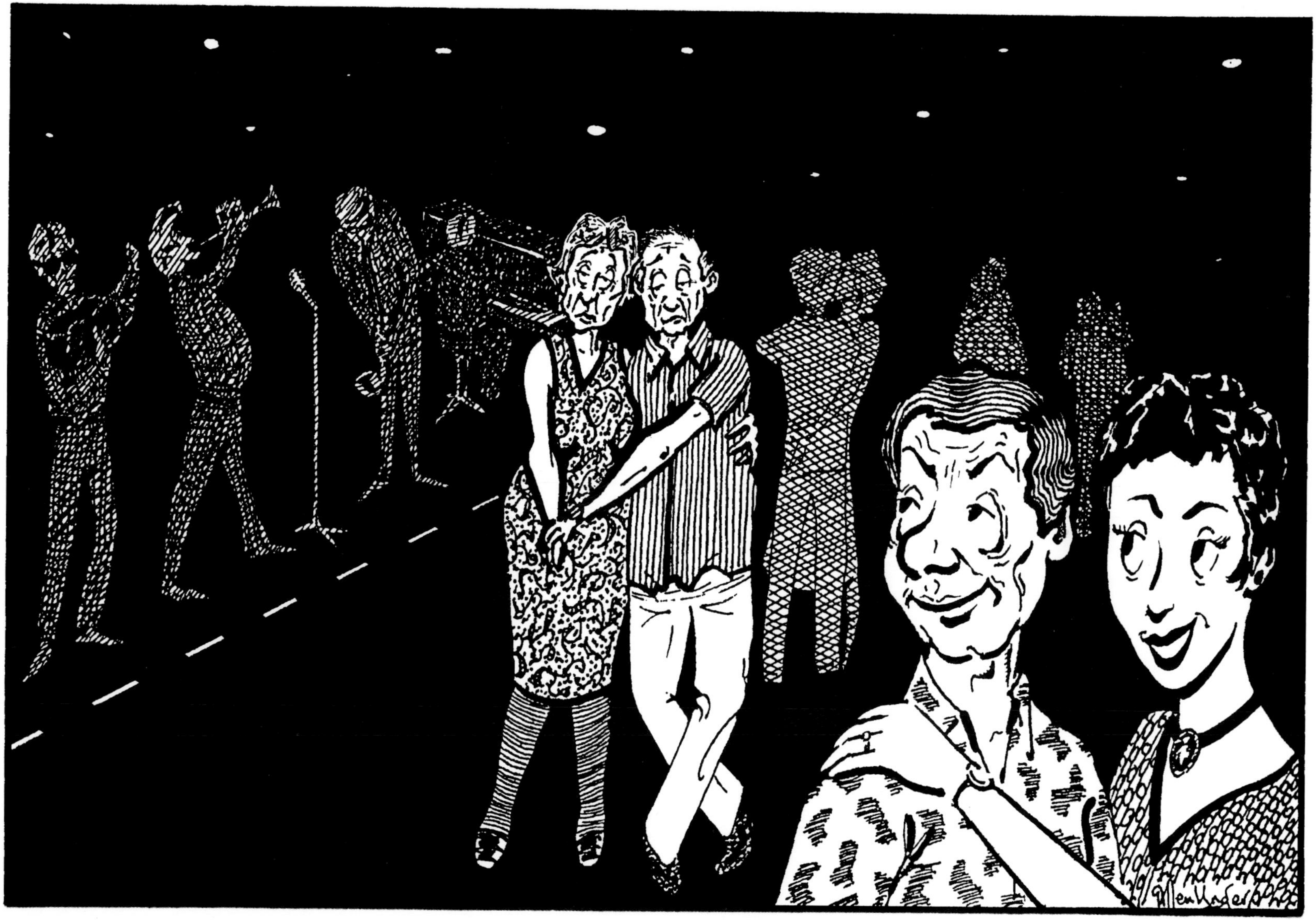

"It's our darling daughter. She hopes we have a great holiday. She says everything is fine at home, and we're not to worry about a thing, and what's the number of the car insurance company?"

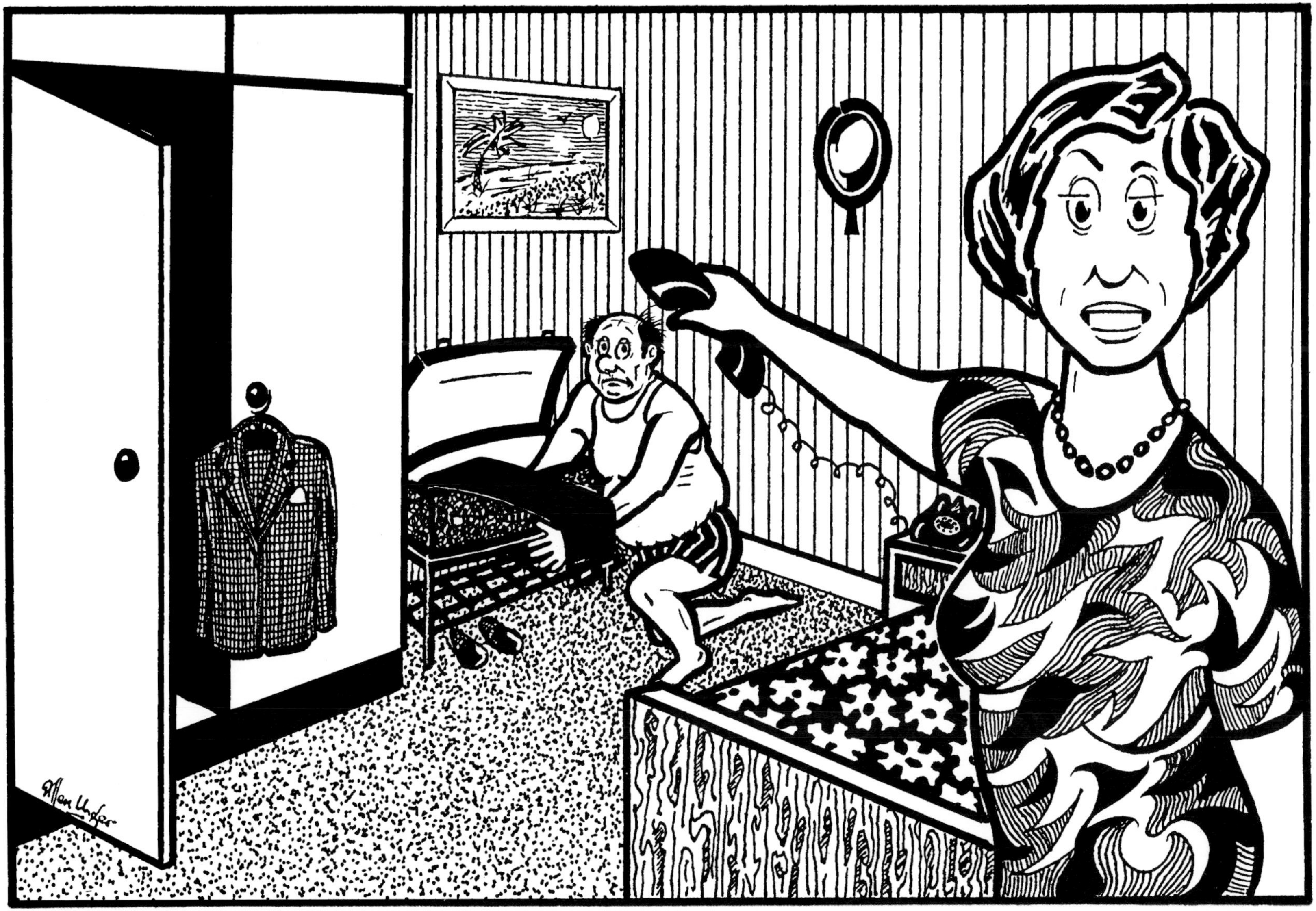

"Your husband's a k'nacker in banking, so I'll explain like this: your gums are not so much in recession as in a complete depression!!!"

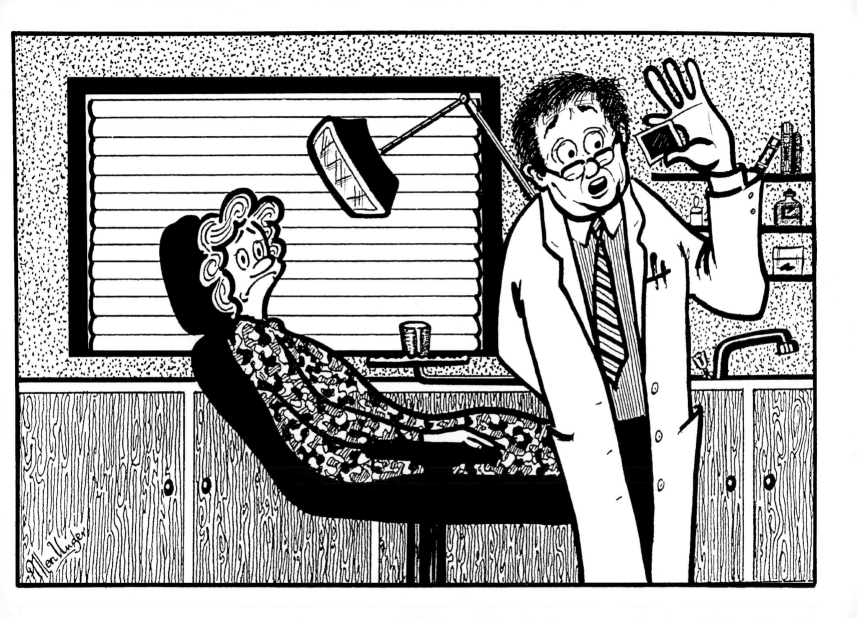

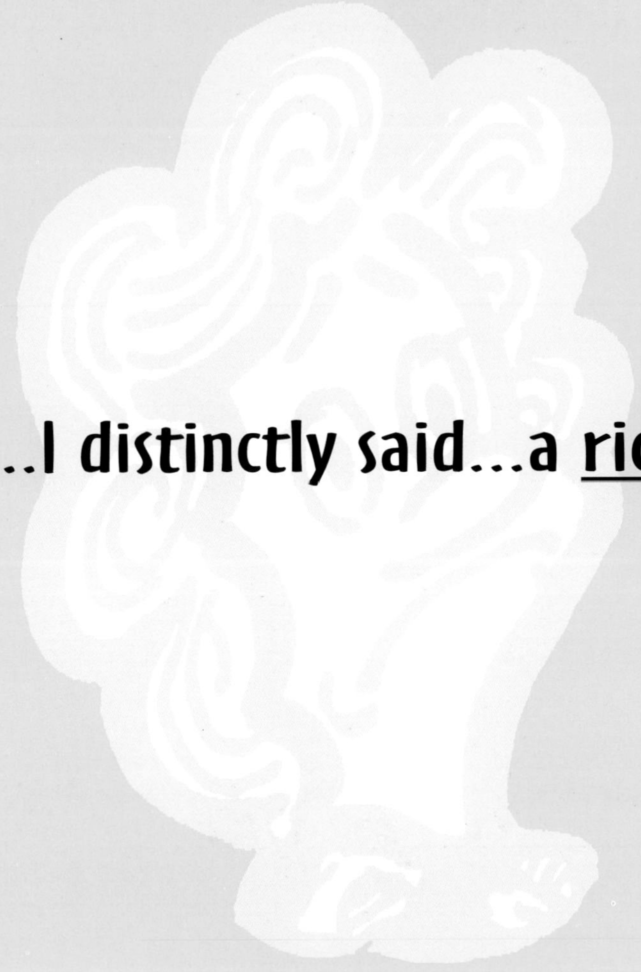

"No Jayne...I distinctly said...a rich doctor!"

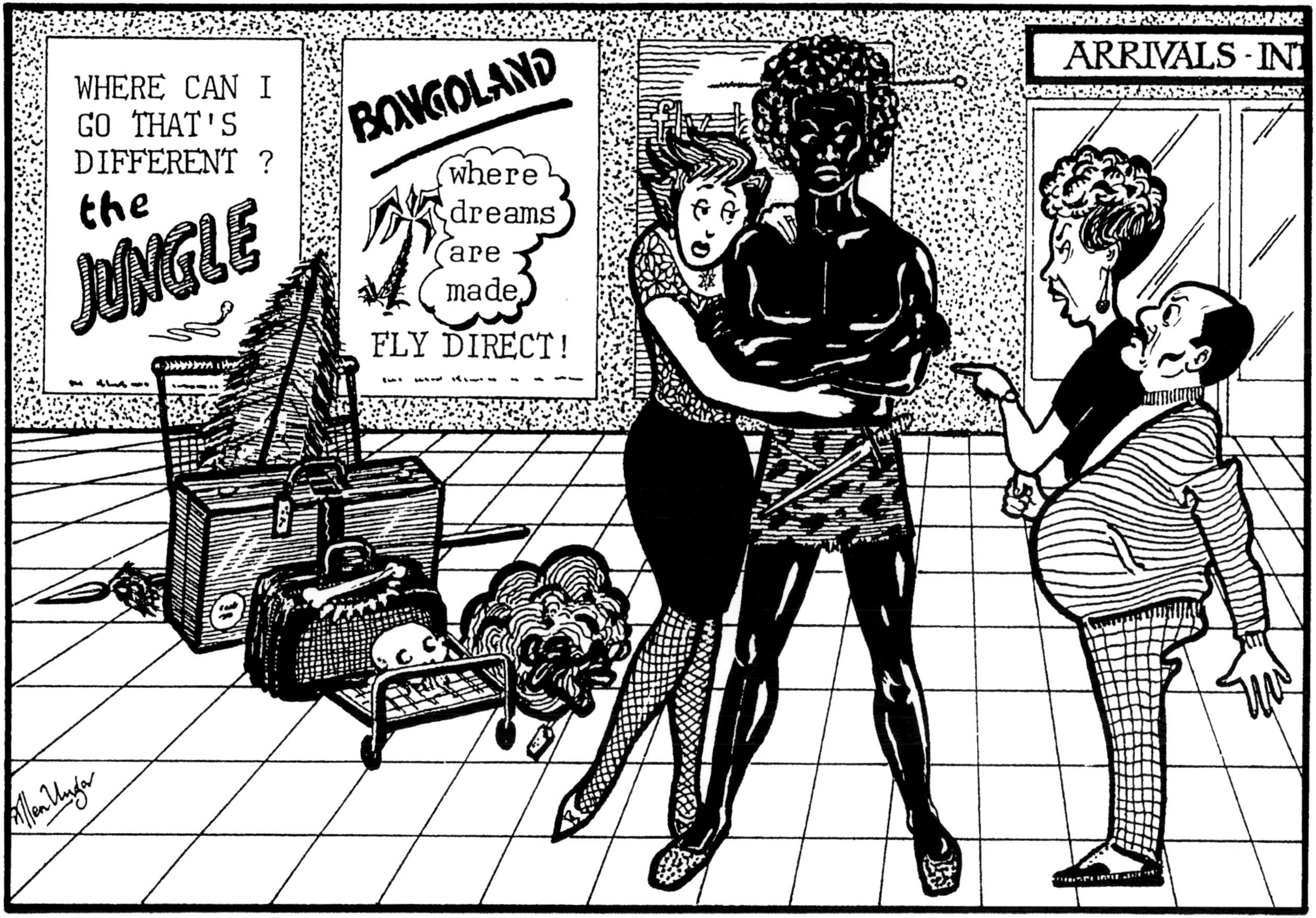
WHERE CAN I GO THAT'S DIFFERENT ?
the JUNGLE
BONGOLAND
where dreams are made
FLY DIRECT!
ARRIVALS - IN
Allen Ungar

"Well, they certainly wouldn't be dressing like that, if they were still our colony!"

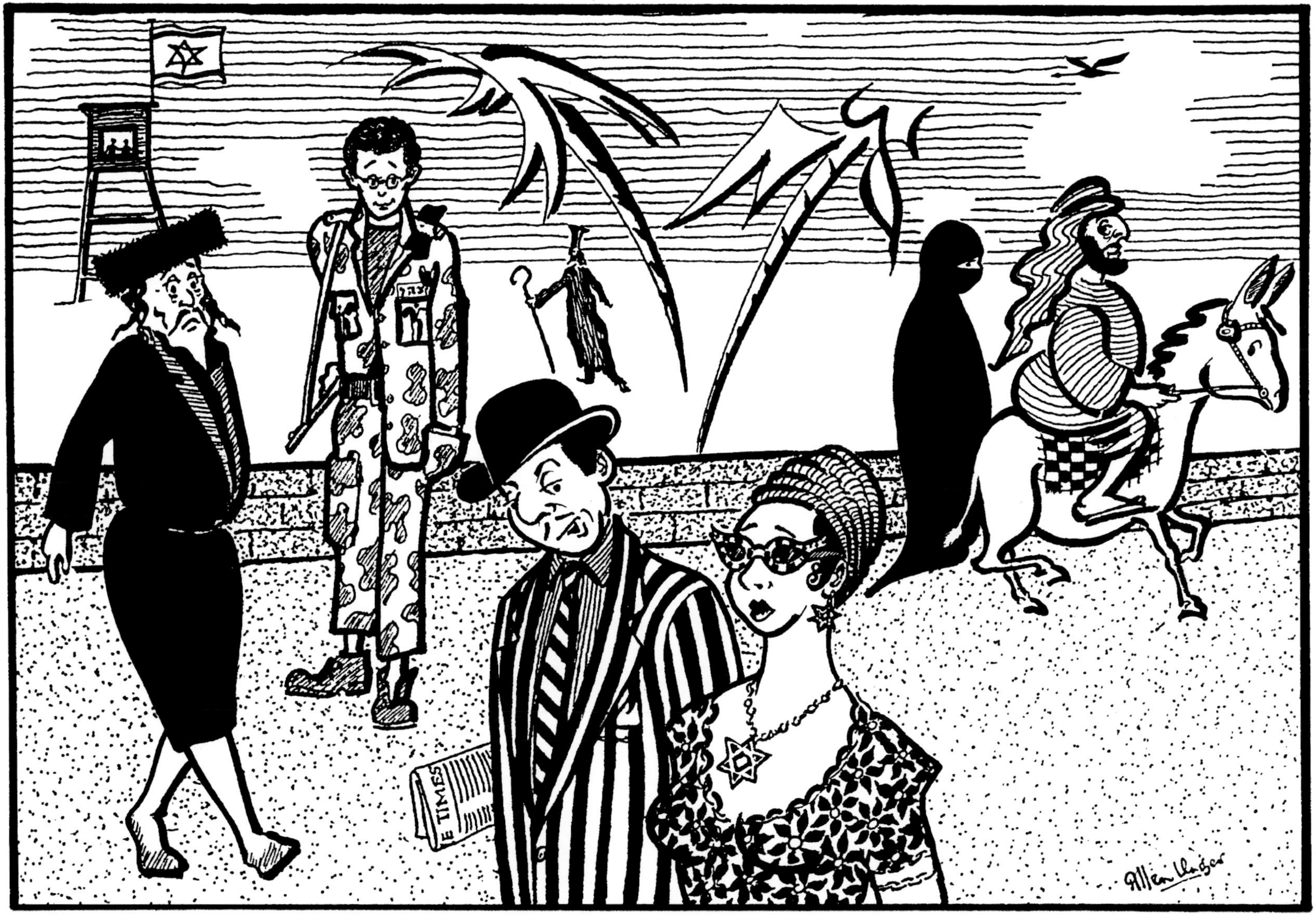
E TIMES
Allen Unger

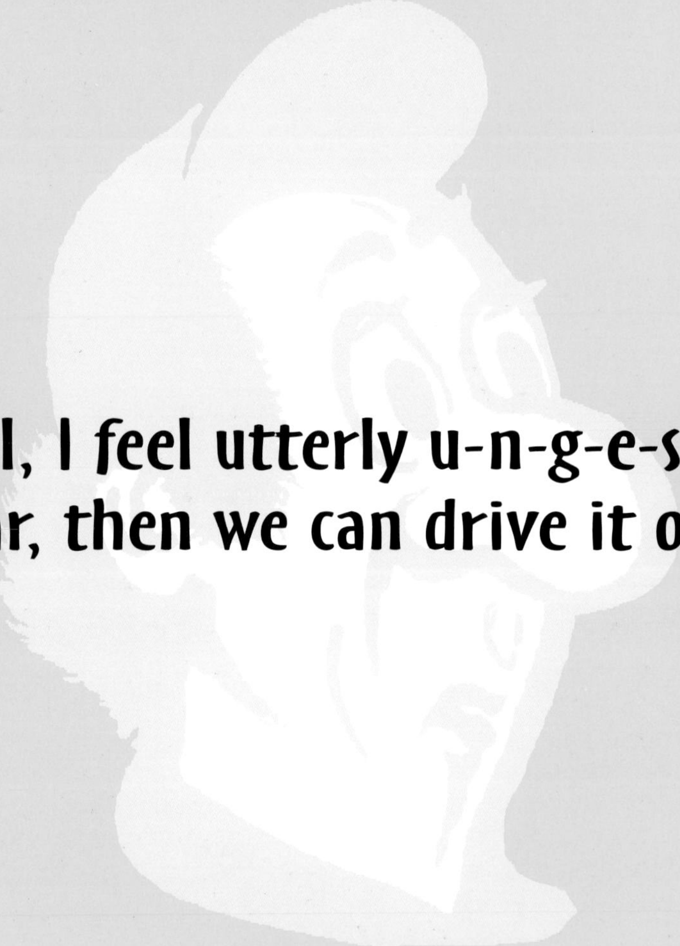

"What a meal, I feel utterly u-n-g-e-s-h-t-o-p-t...
I'll get the car, then we can drive it off."

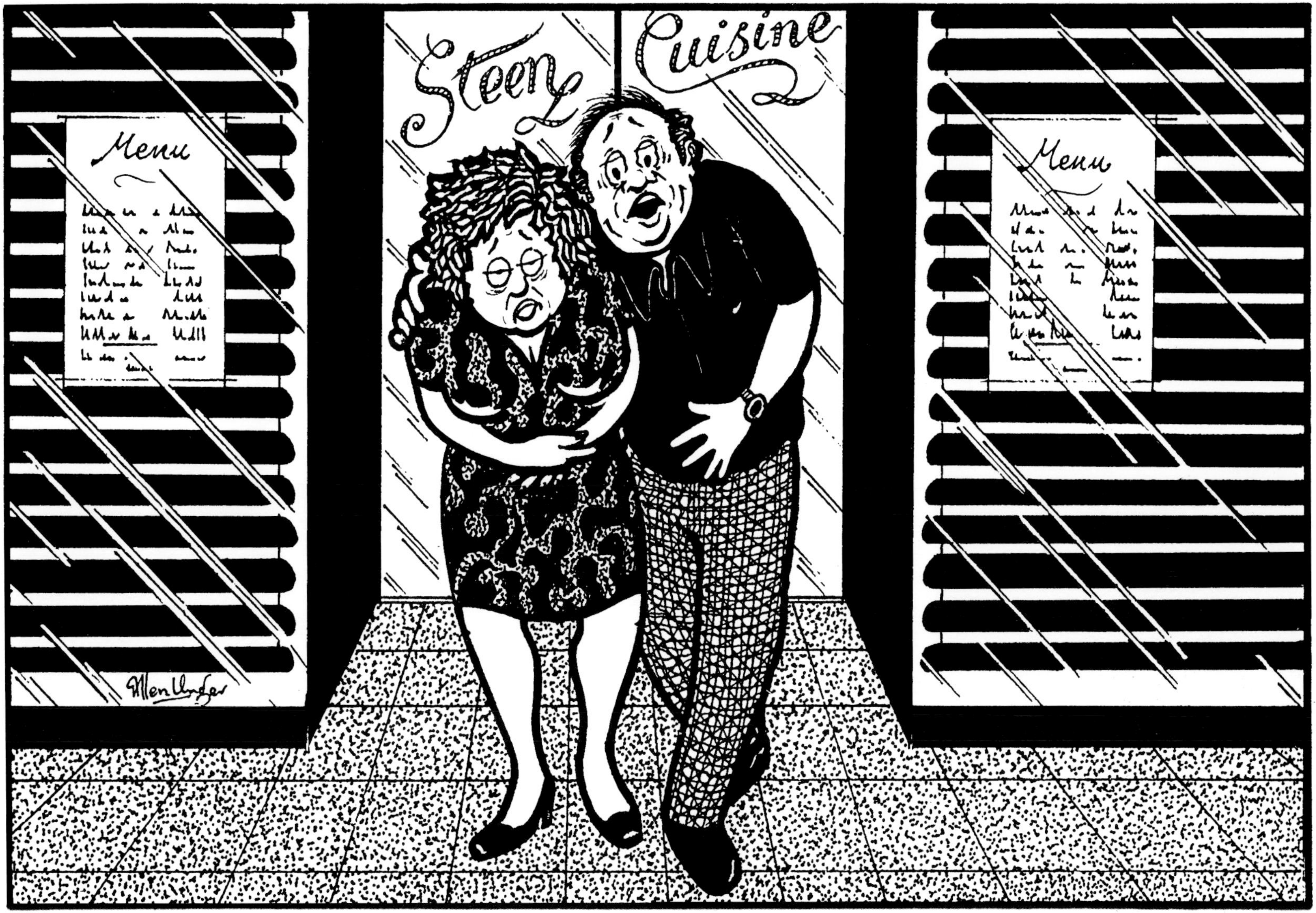
Steen Cuisine
Menu
Menu

"We're only on half board, so get six more bagels, jelly, butter, and a schmeer...oh yes, some lox...and then we'll have enough for lunch. Drinks we can buy."

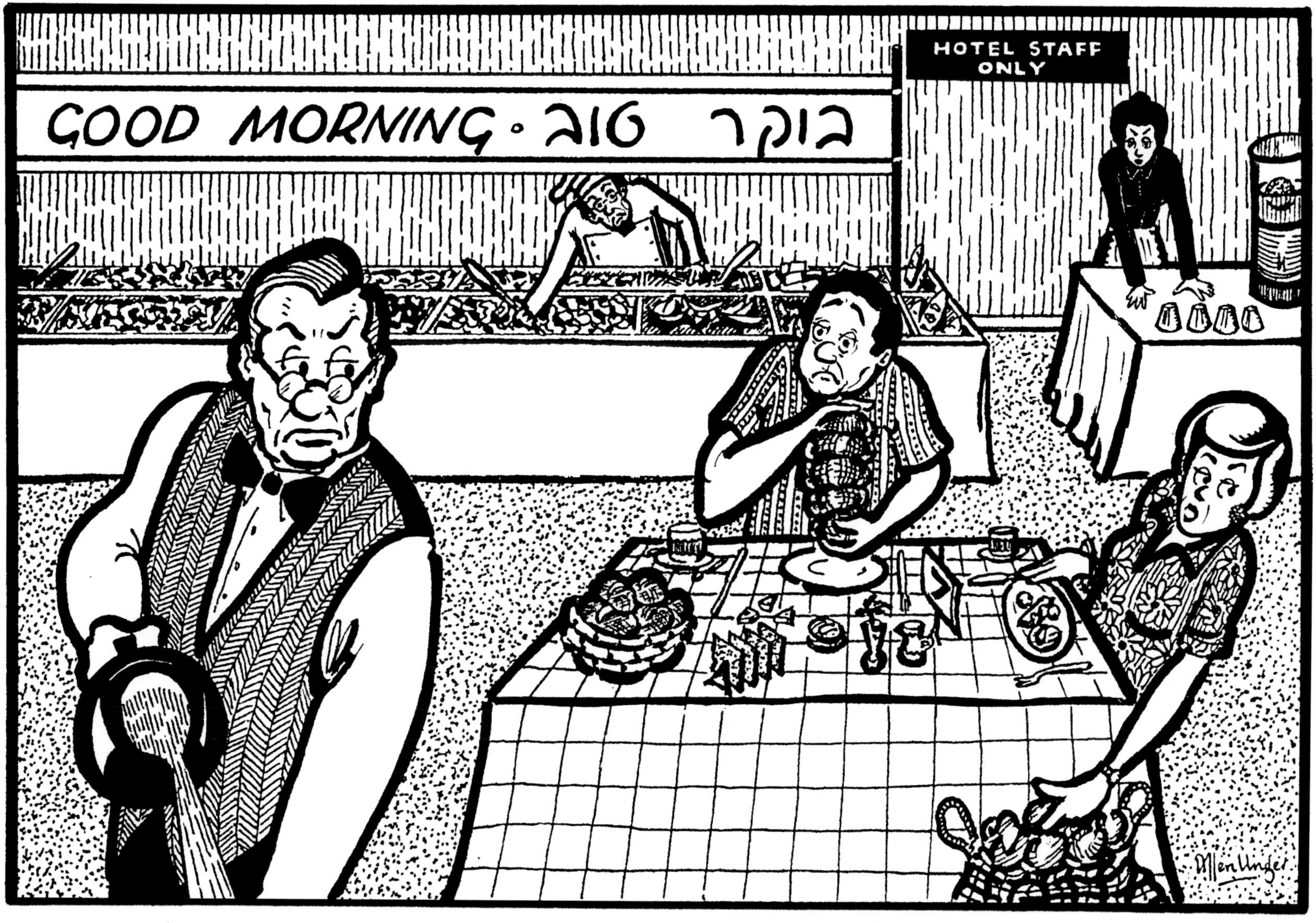
HOTEL STAFF
ONLY
GOOD MORNING • בוקר טוב

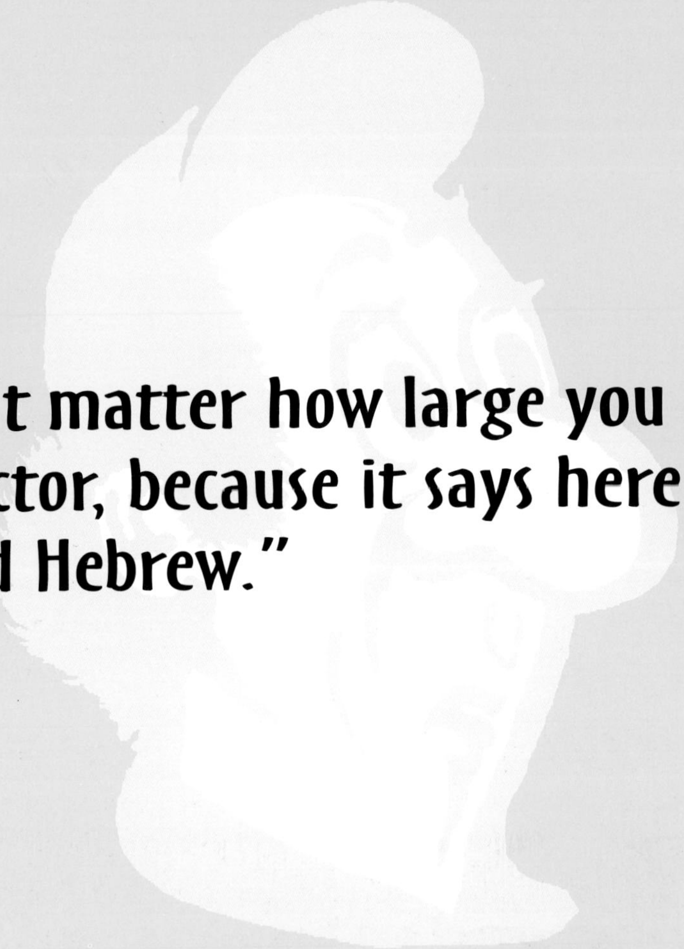

"It doesn't matter how large you make the letter, doctor, because it says here that he can't read Hebrew."

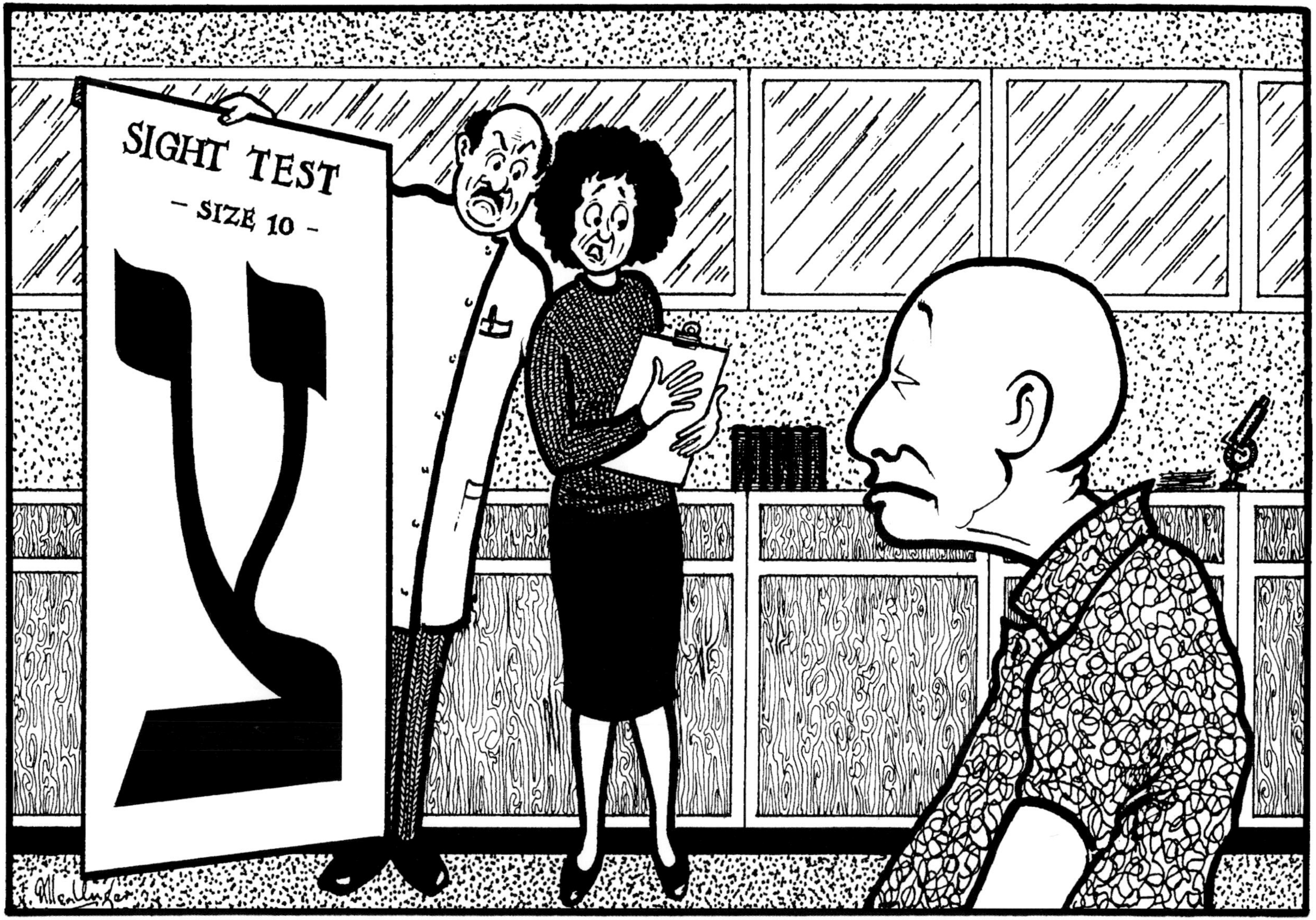
SIGHT TEST
– SIZE 10 –
ע

"Mr. Rosenberg, a customer wants his photograph taken to send to a schadchan, I wouldn't waste your time showing him wedding albums."

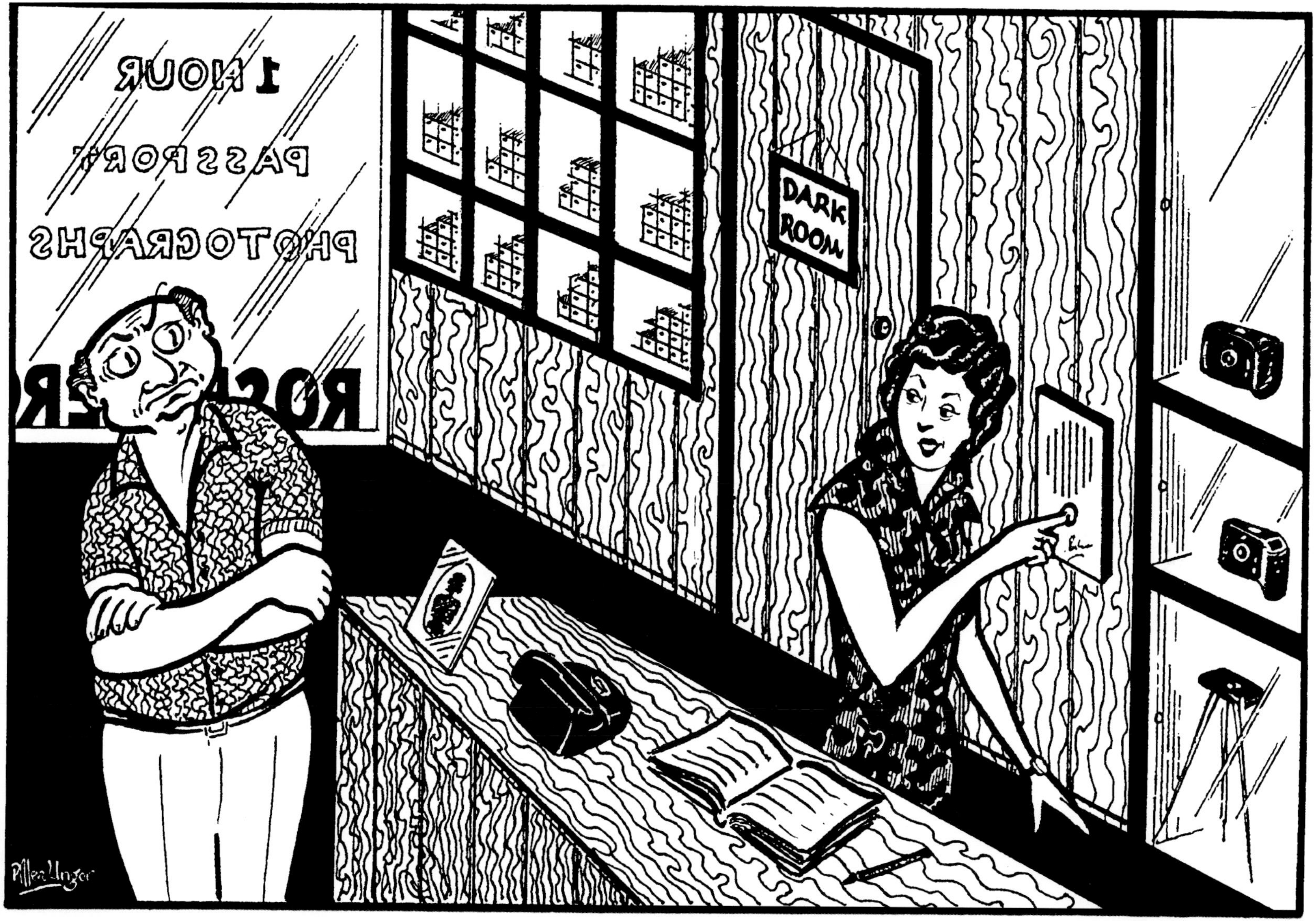
1 HOUR
PASSPORT
PHOTOGRAPHS
DARK ROOM
Allen Unger

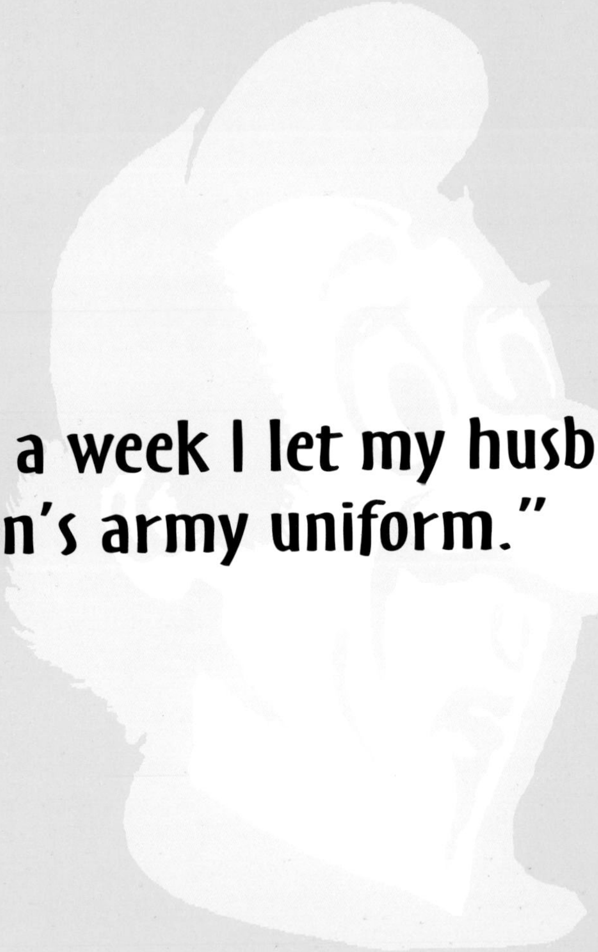

"Once a week I let my husband wear our son's army uniform."

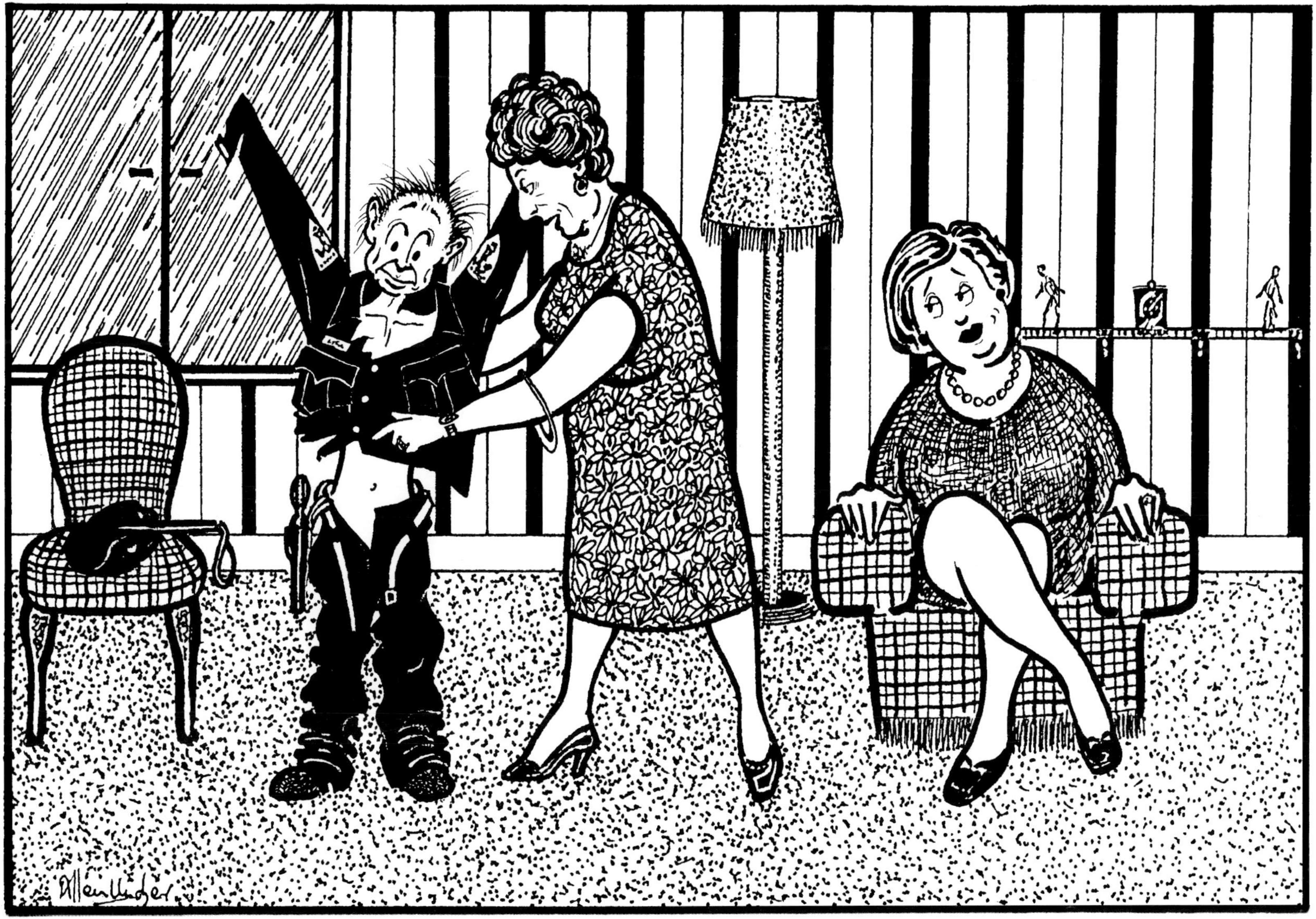
D Allen Unger

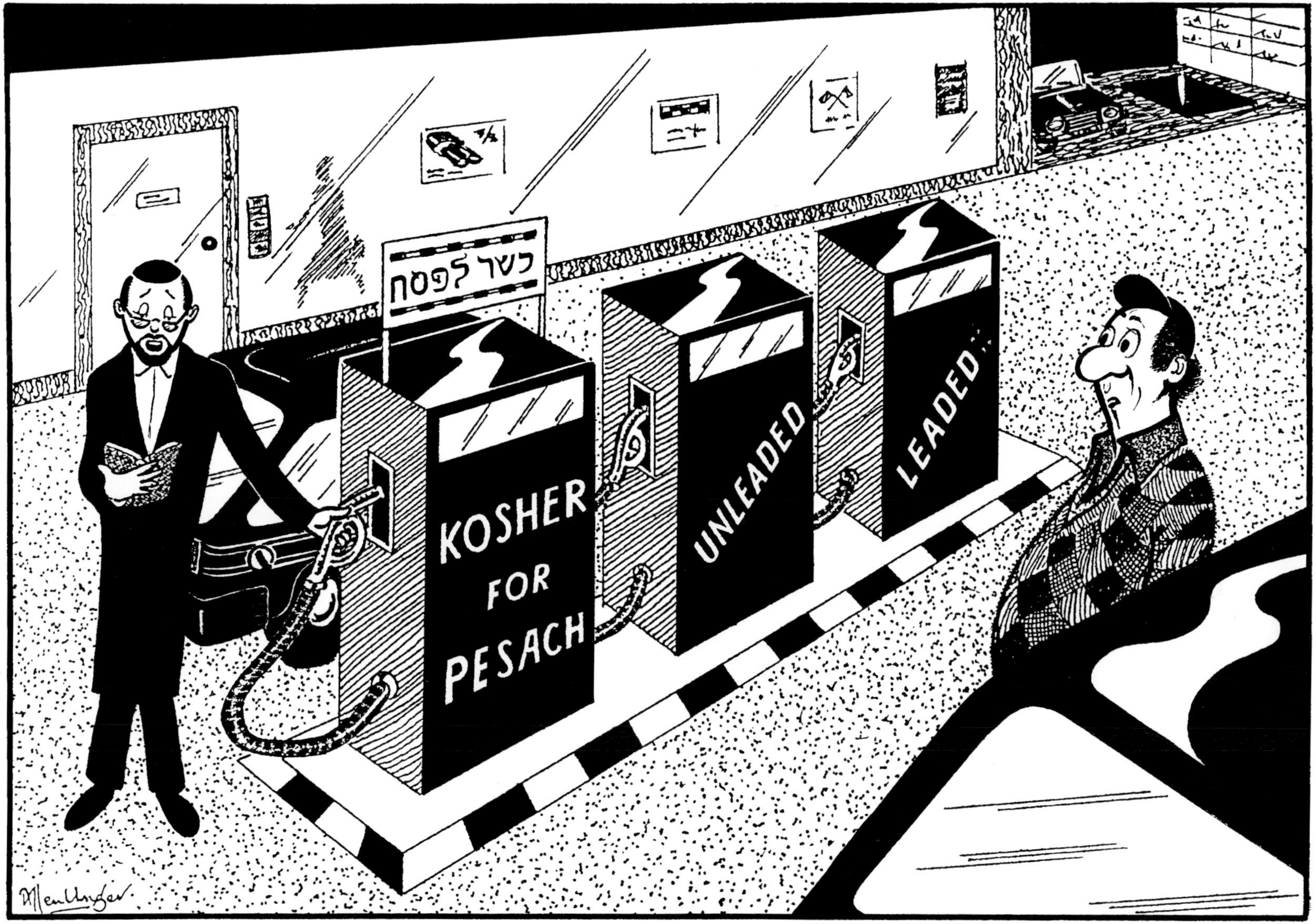
כשר לפסח
KOSHER FOR PESACH
UNLEADED
LEADED
Allen Unger

"The last time I saw him beg like that was when his wife told him that she was pregnant again...after the nine daughters."

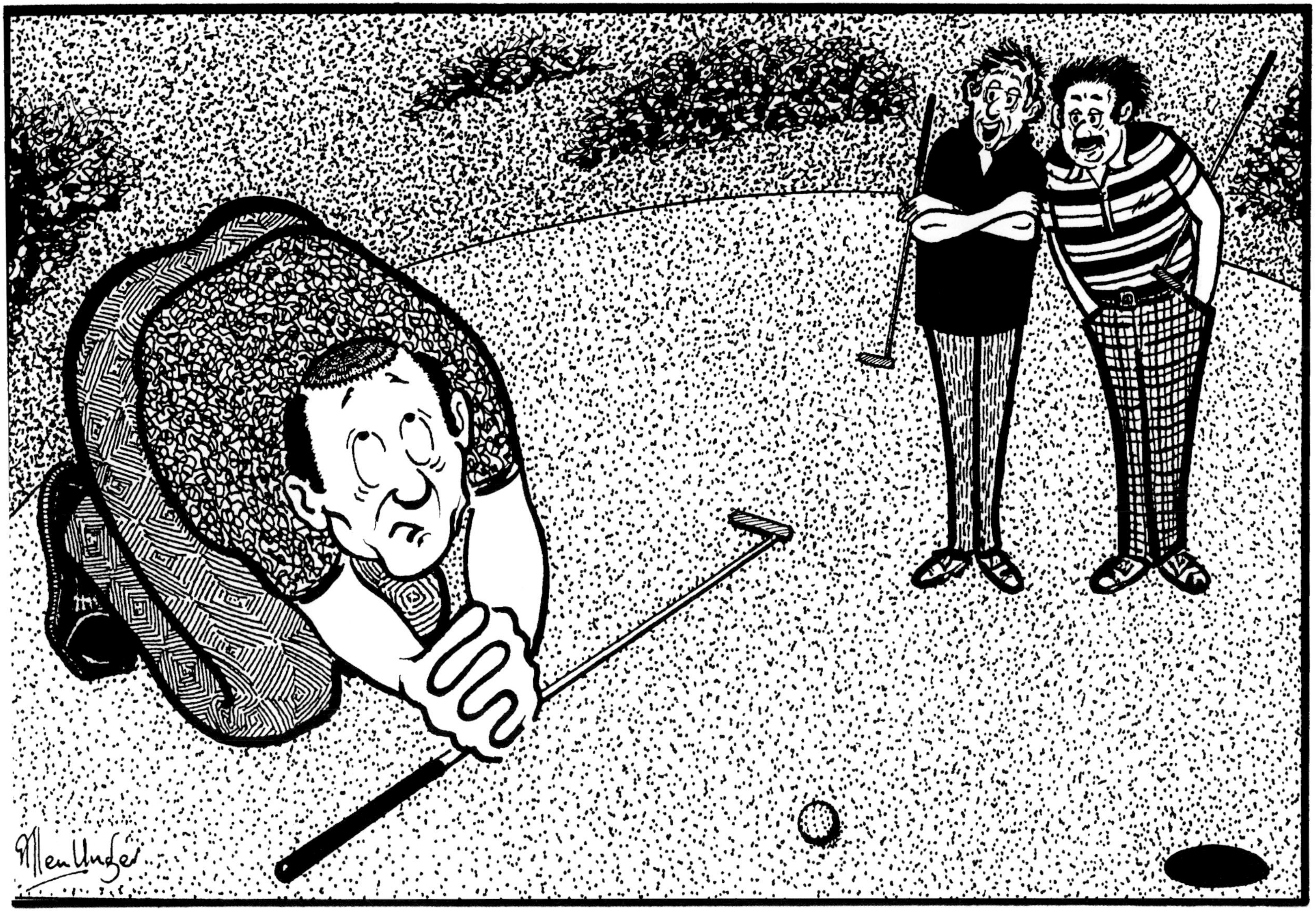

"Sid, come quickly...this isn't another one of my bubba-maysahs."

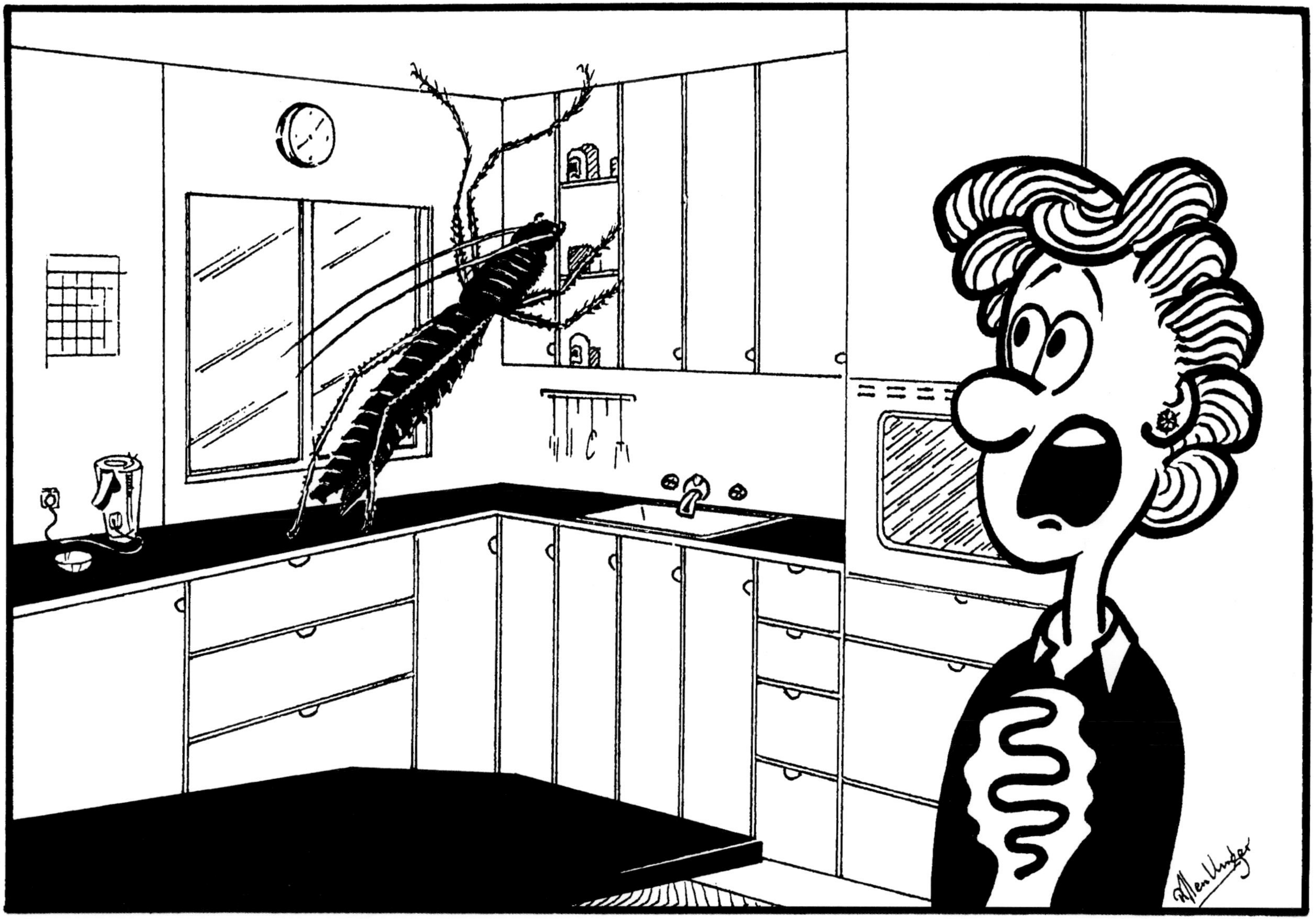

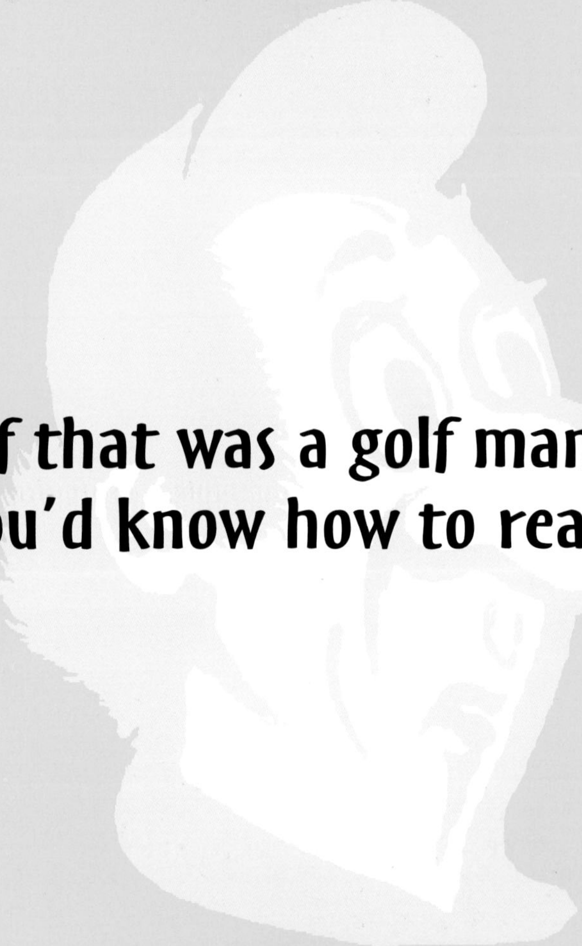

"If that was a golf manual,
you'd know how to read it."

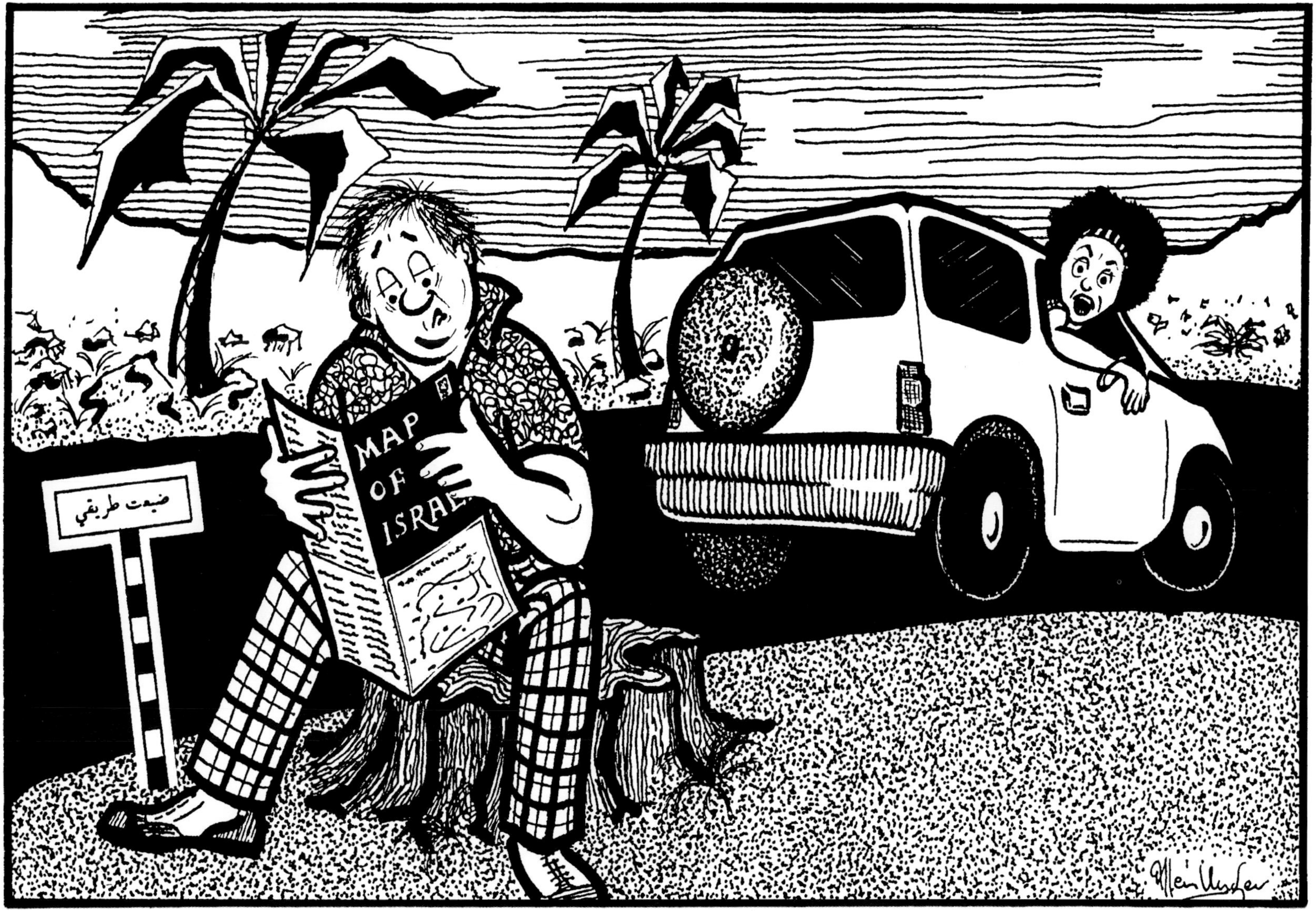
ضيعت طريقي
MAP OF ISRAEL

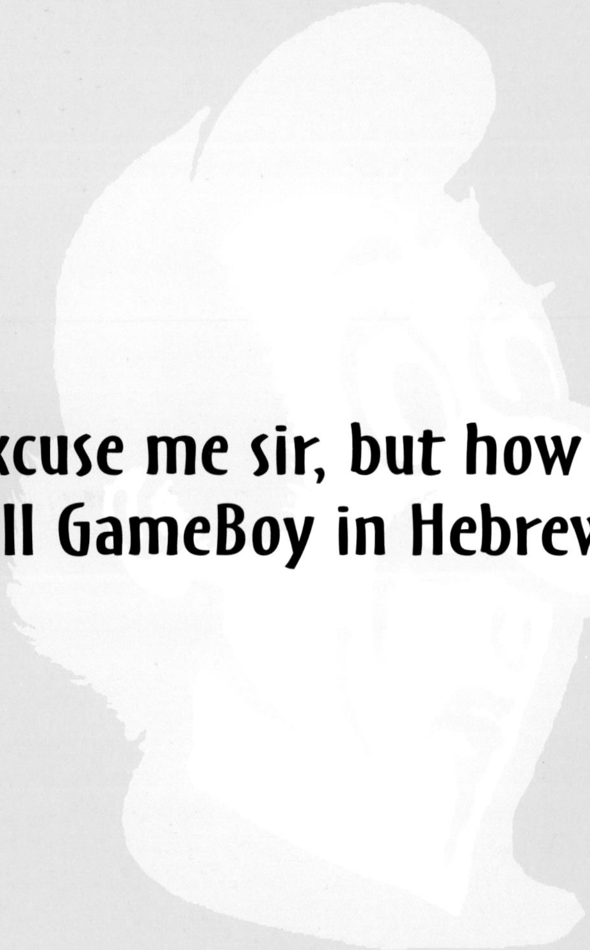

"Excuse me sir, but how do you spell GameBoy in Hebrew?"

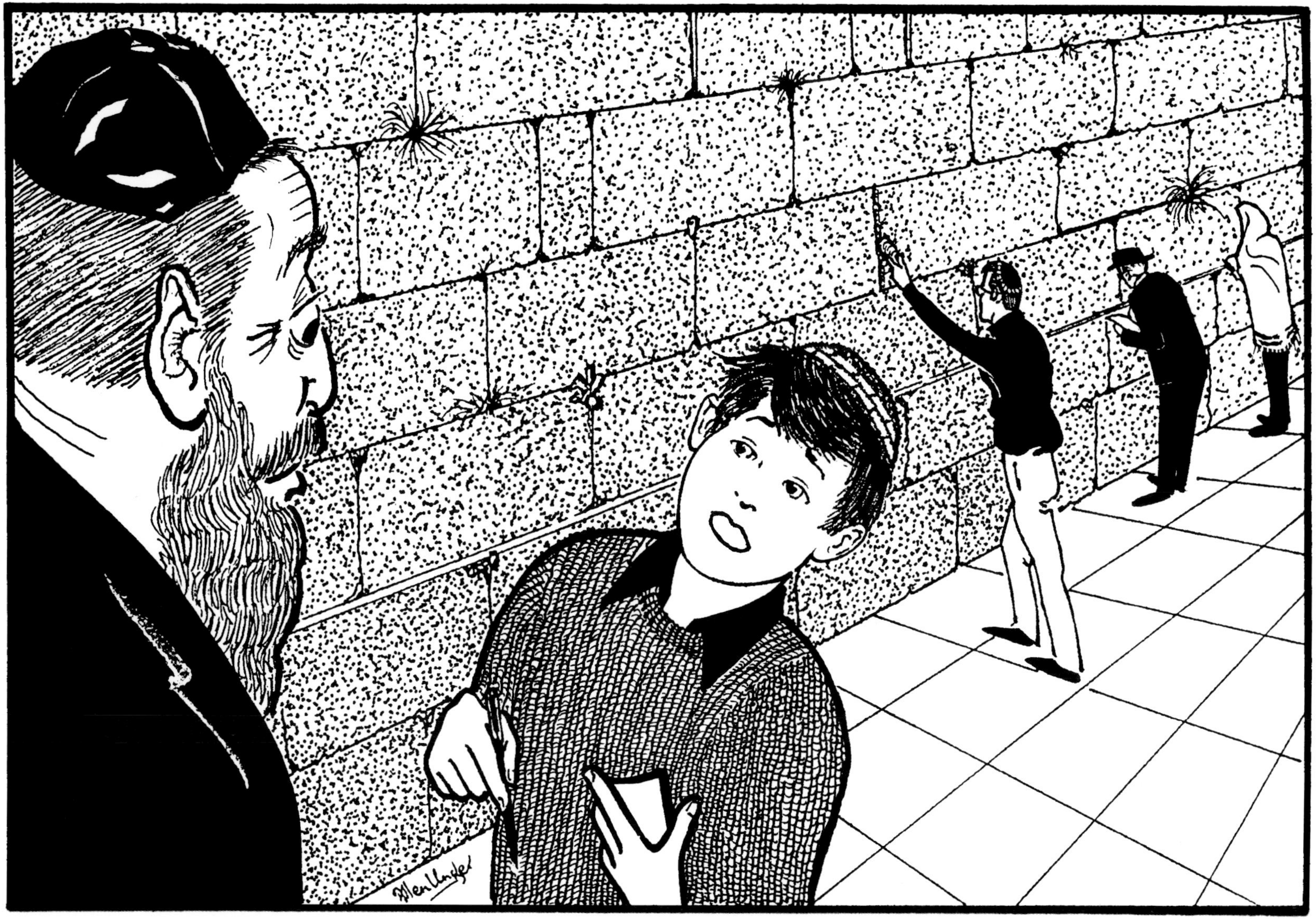

"Out you come sweetheart, you are beginning to look like a cholent in a swimsuit."

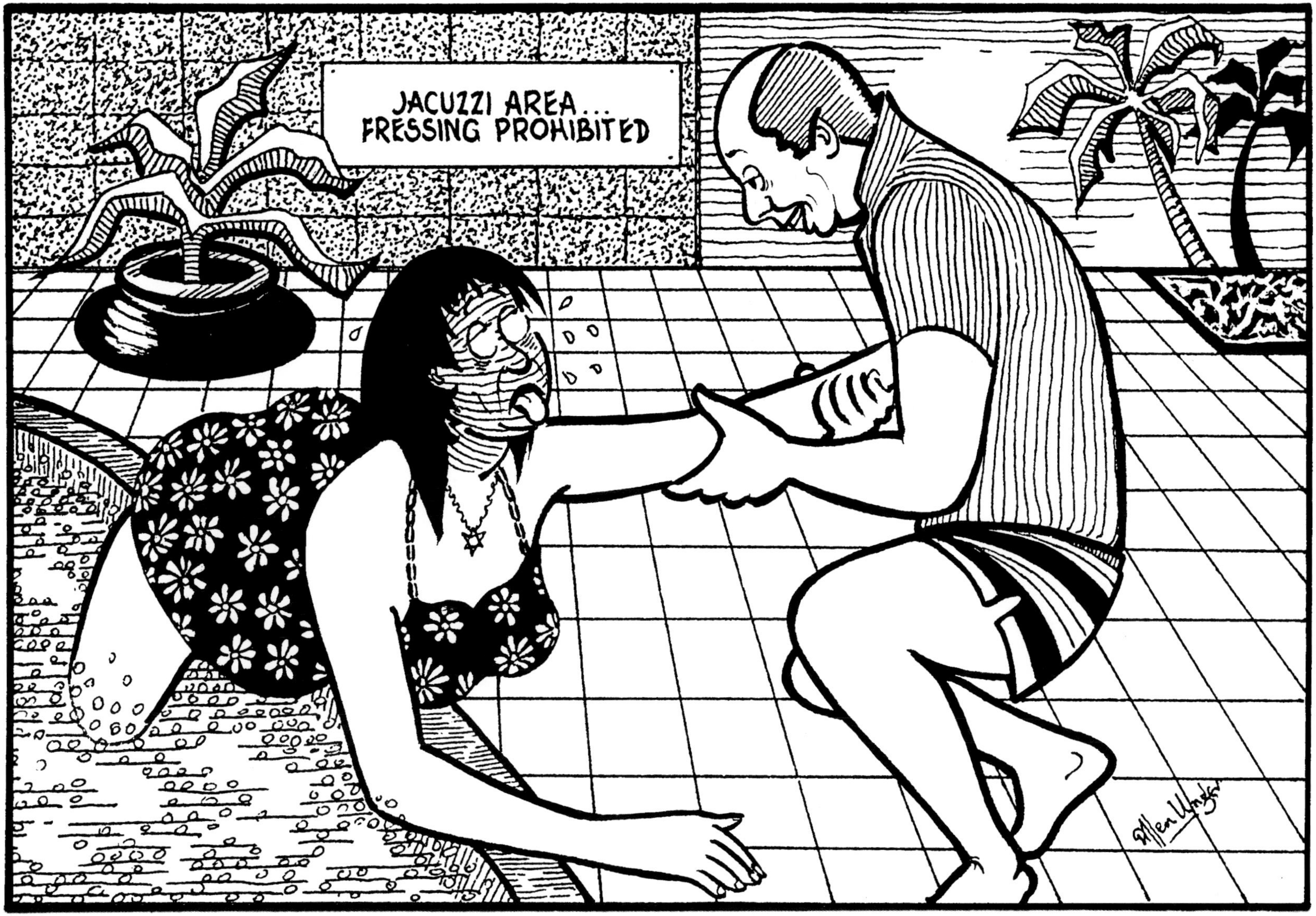
JACUZZI AREA...
FRESSING PROHIBITED

"It says here that Lot's wife turned into a pillar of salt near this spot, because she couldn't keep her eyes to herself!"

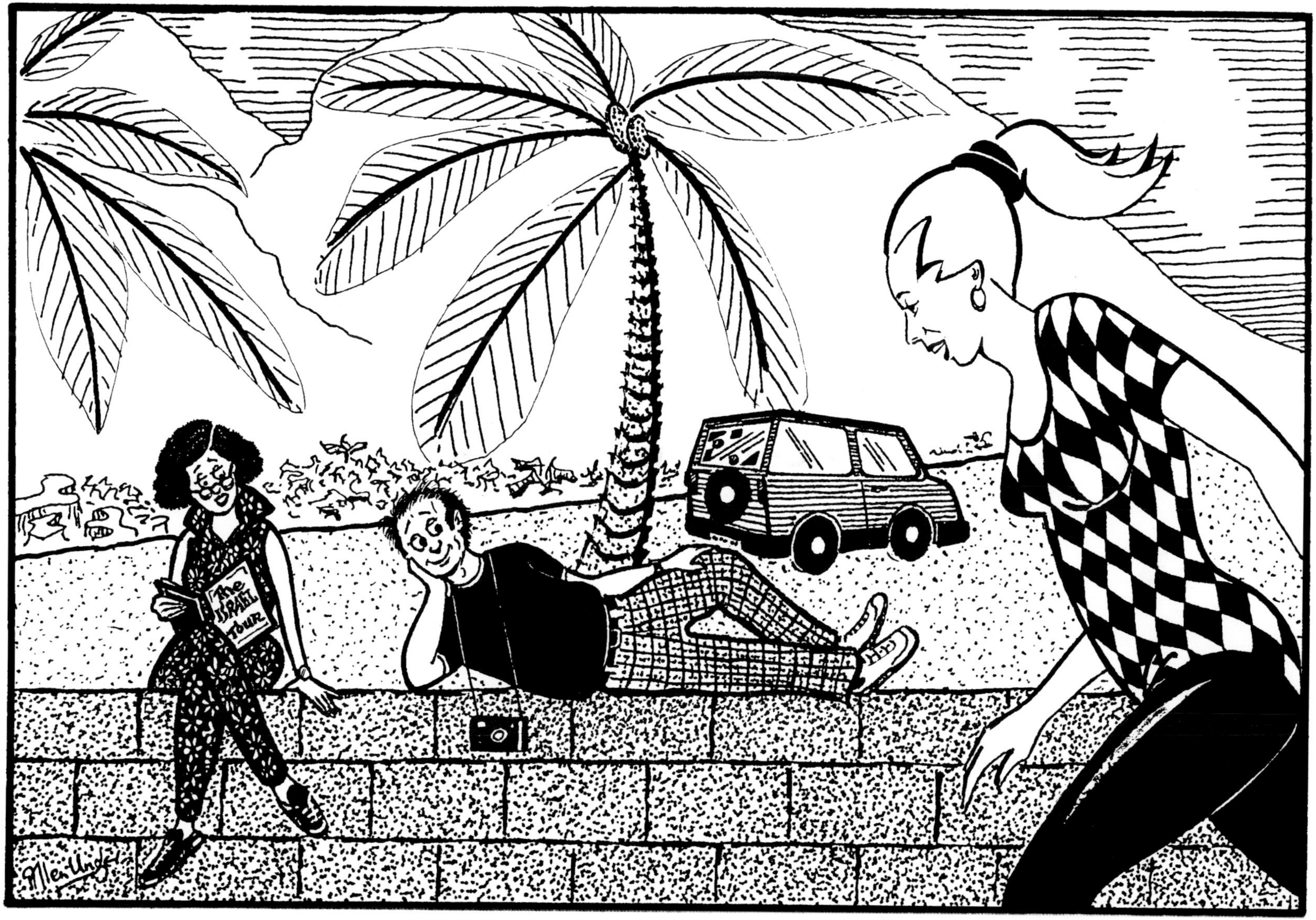
The ISRAEL TOUR

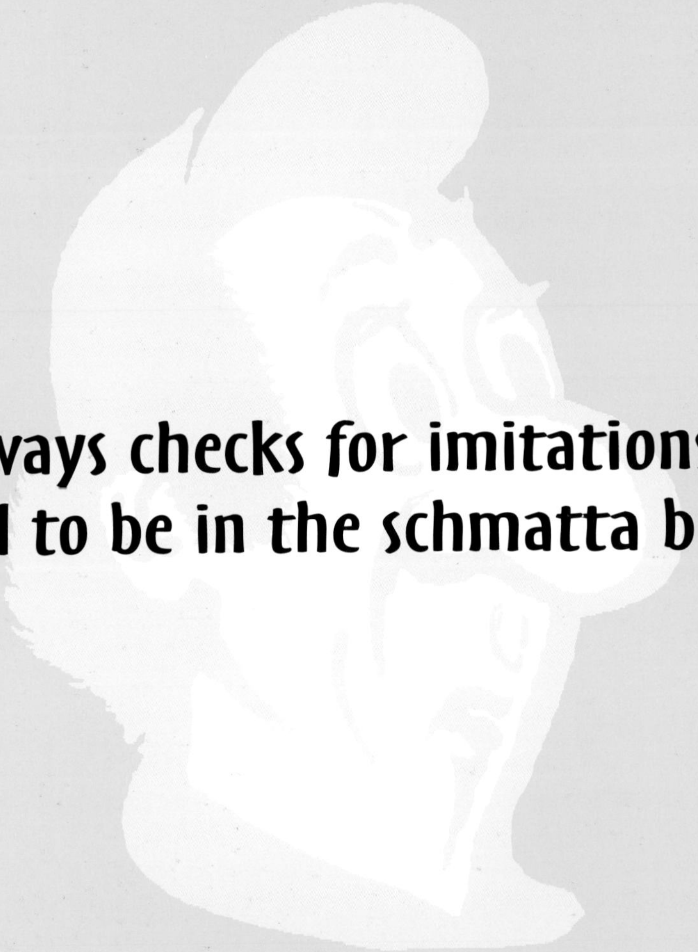

"He always checks for imitations,
he used to be in the schmatta business."

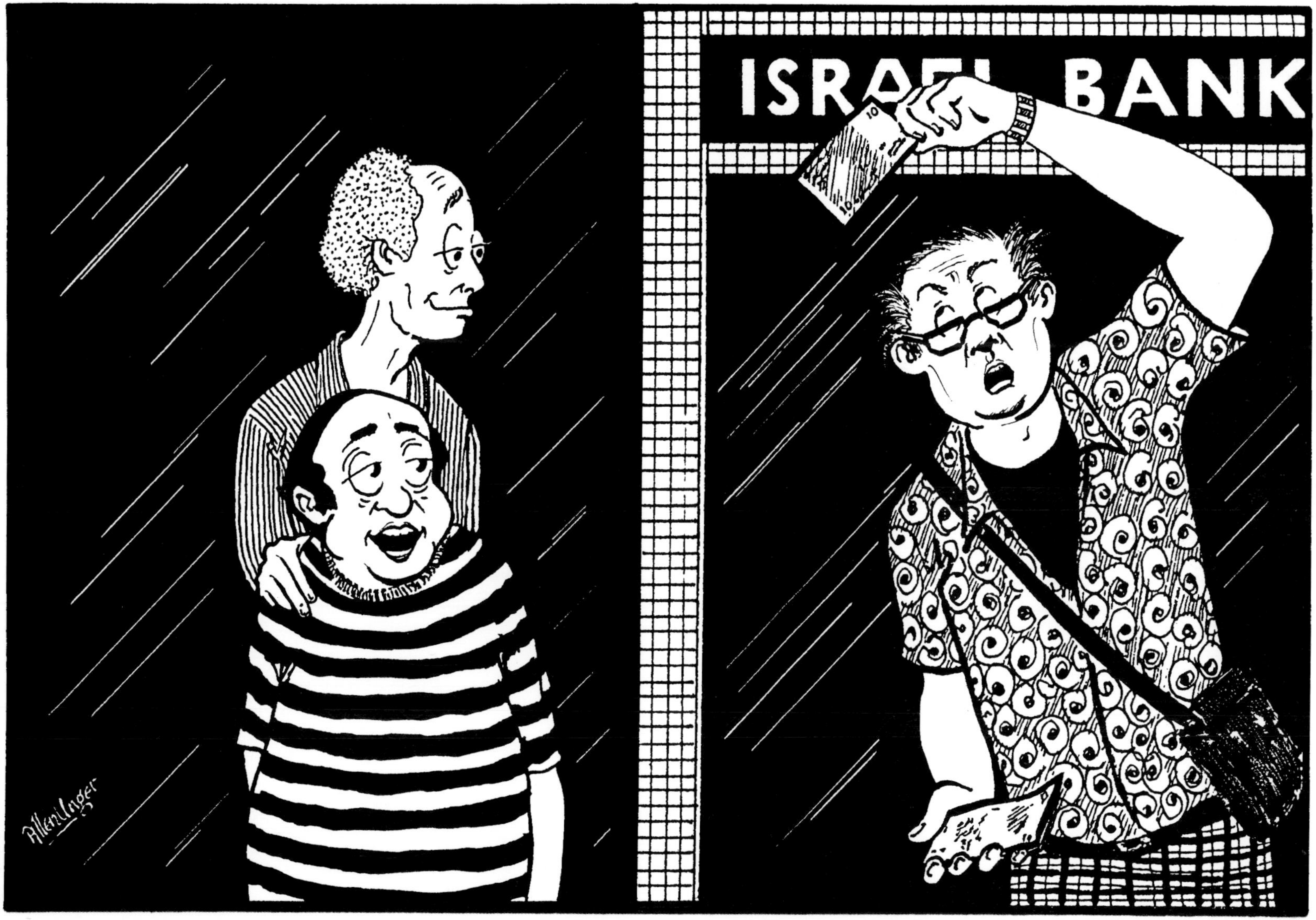
ISRAEL BANK

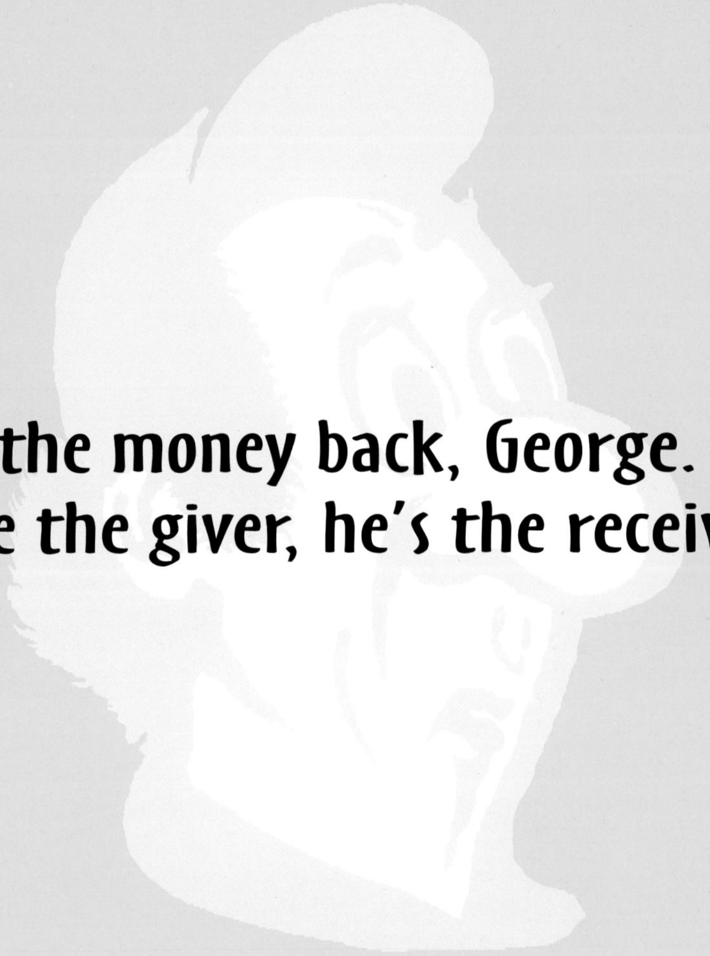

"Put the money back, George.
You're the giver, he's the receiver!"

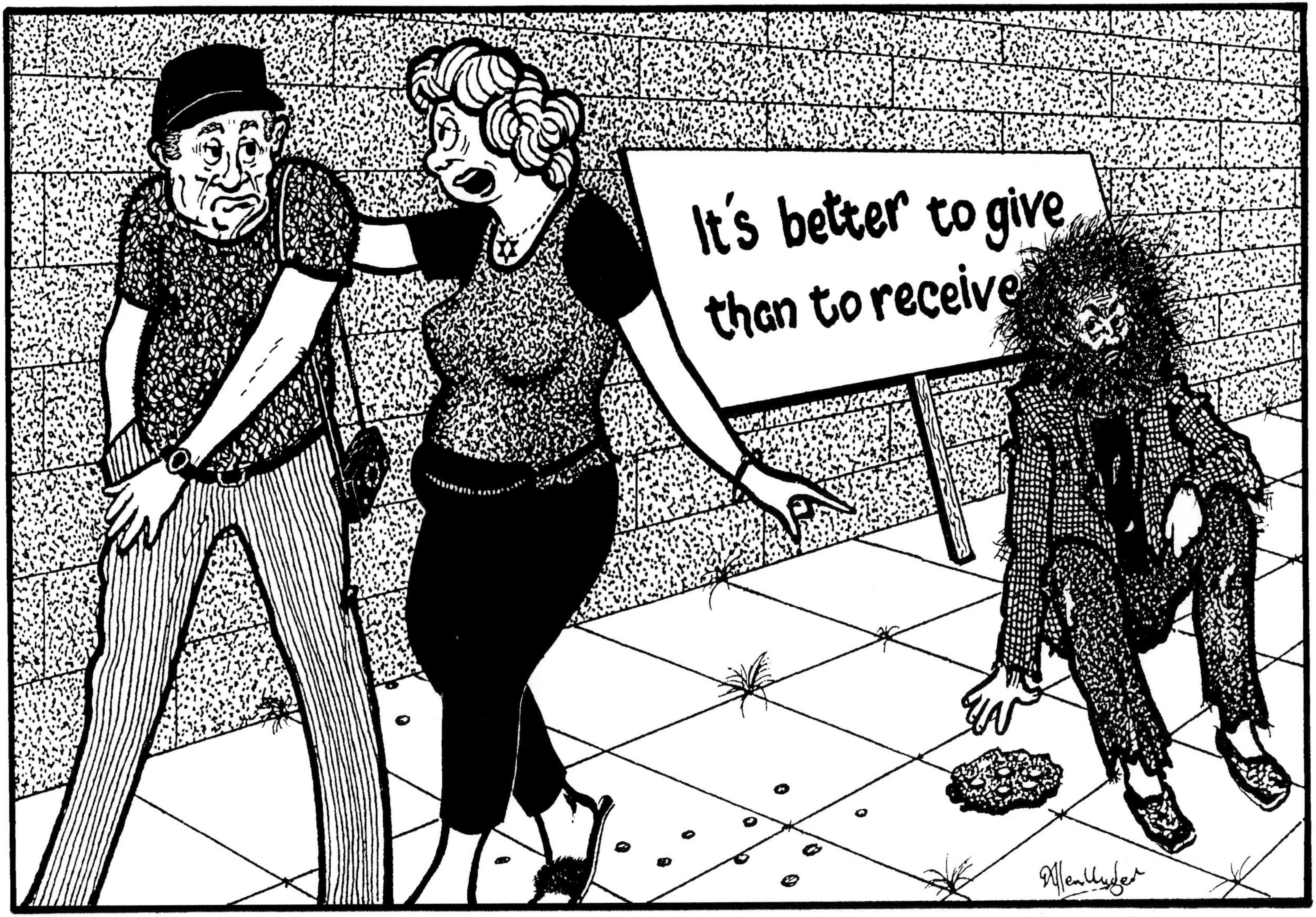
It's better to give
than to receive

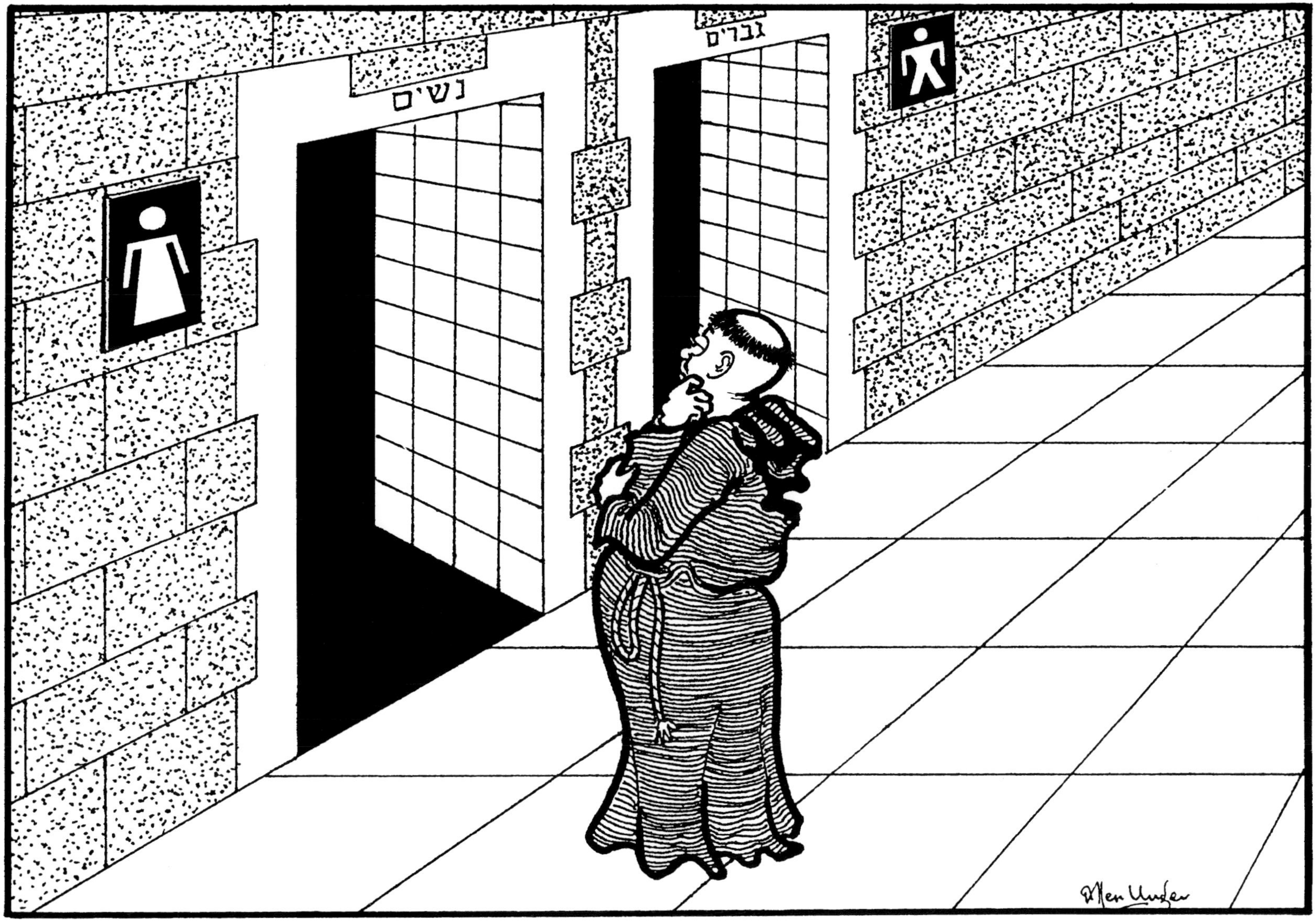
נשים
גברים

"Hershel, tell this bulvan who cut in, that in a minute you'll give him an evil eye he'll never forget!"

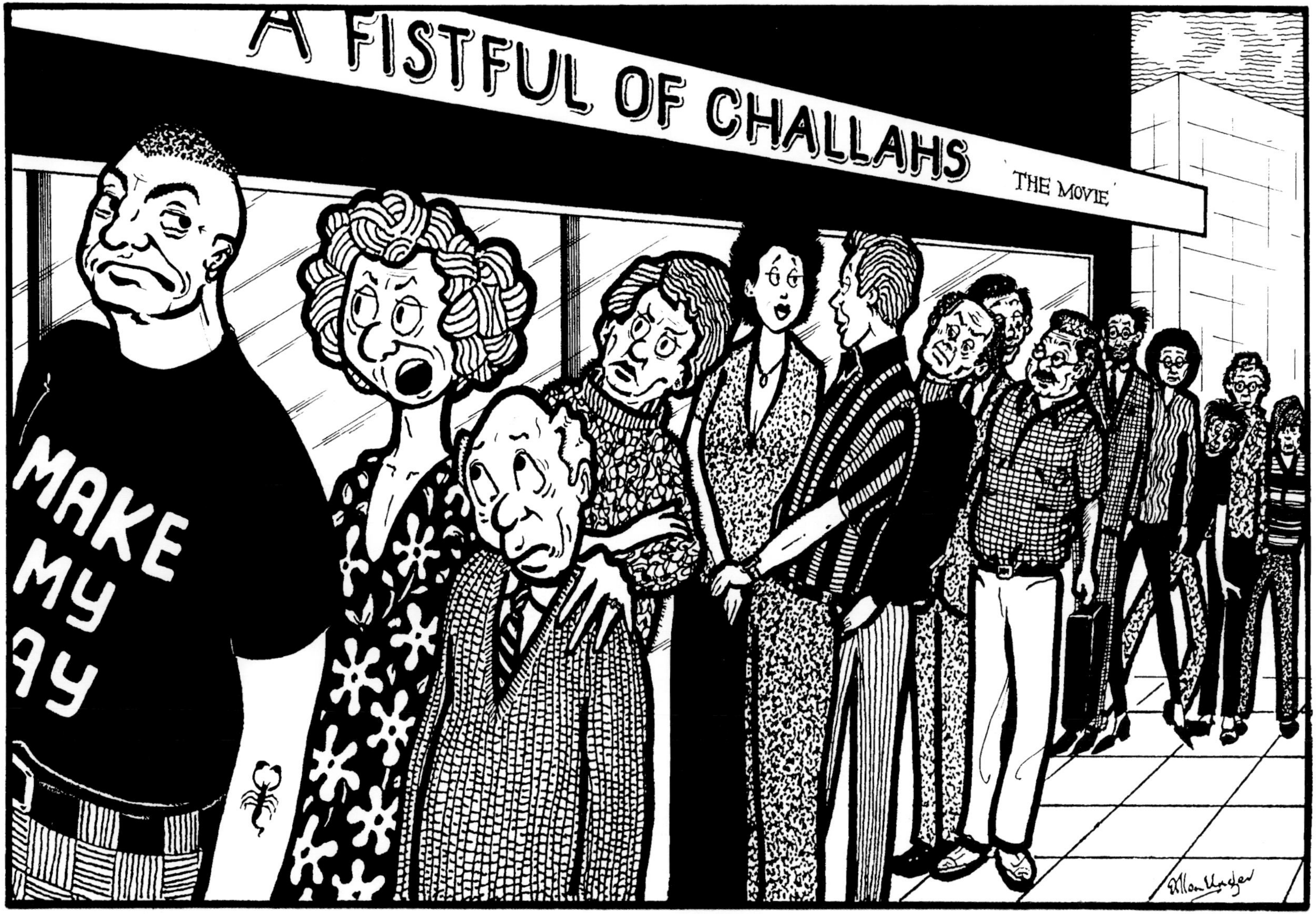
A FISTFUL OF CHALLAHS
THE MOVIE
MAKE
MY
AY

"We have the ultra-orthodox and the secular, the Hizbollah and the Fatah, not to mention the intifada...so who needs you two?"

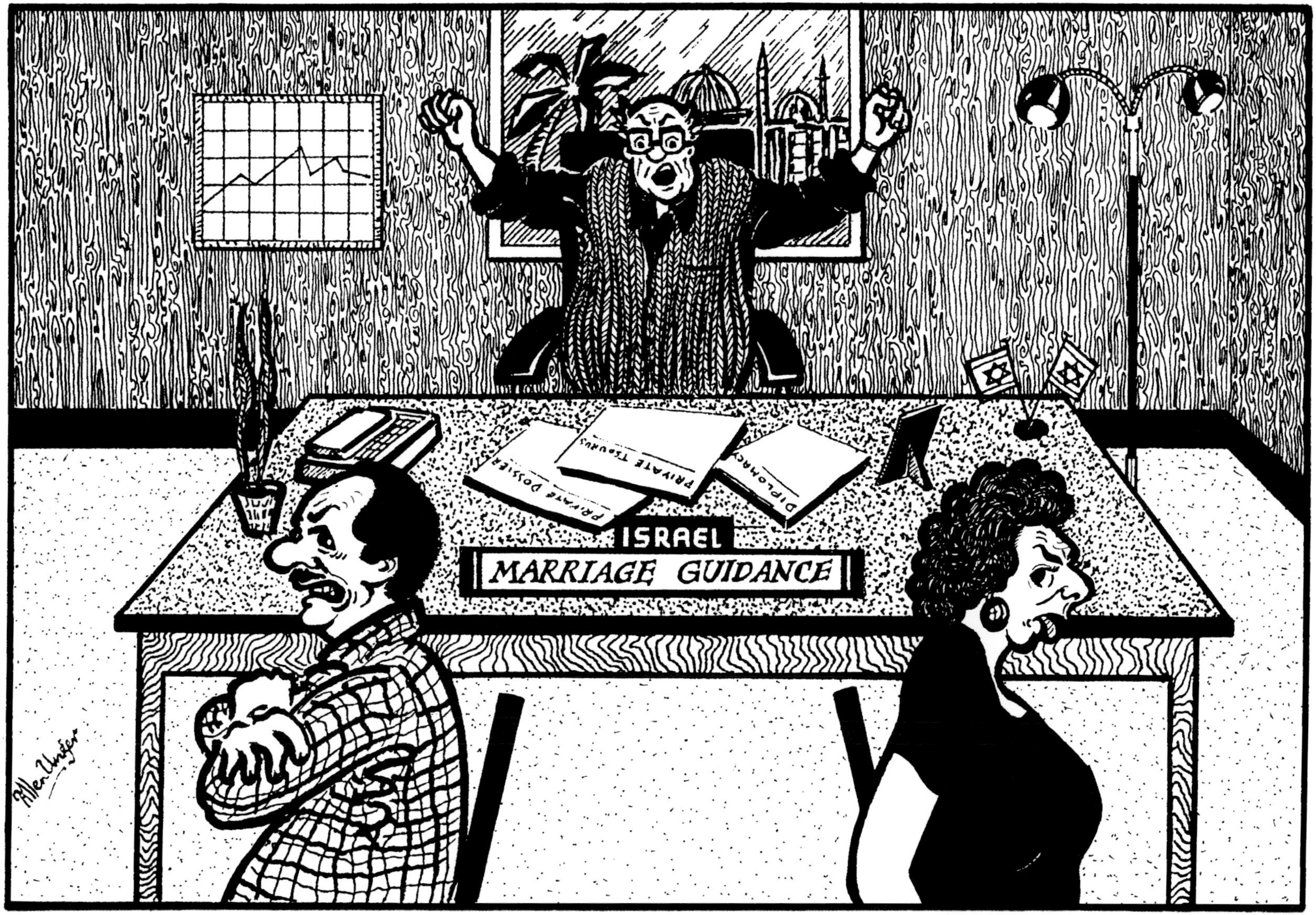
PRIVATE DOSSIER
PRIVATE TSOURUS
DIPLOMACY
ISRAEL
MARRIAGE GUIDANCE
Allen Unger

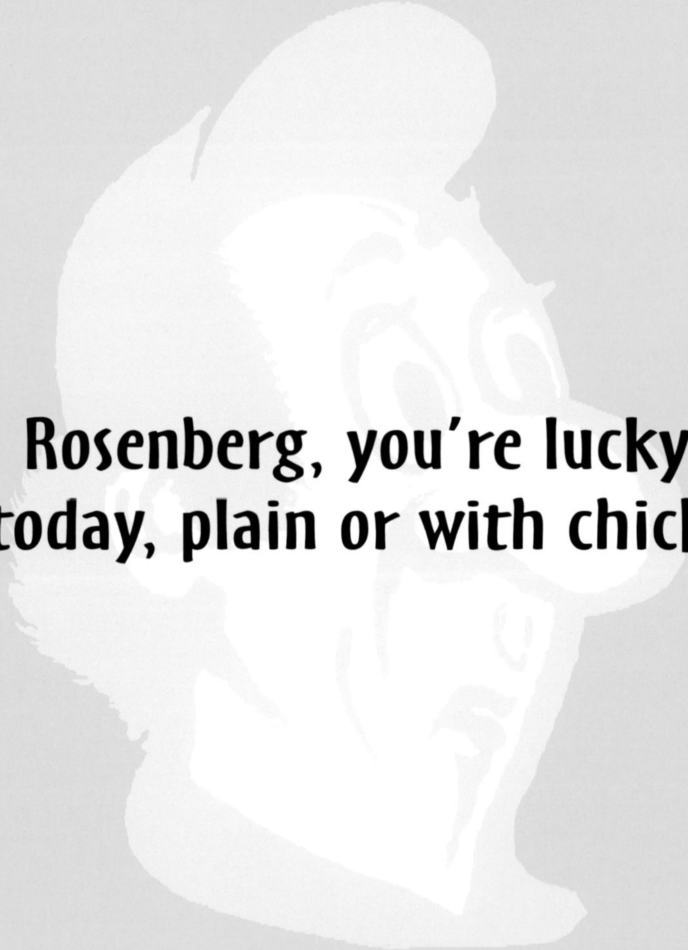

"Well, Mr. Rosenberg, you're lucky, we have a special today, plain or with chicken soup."

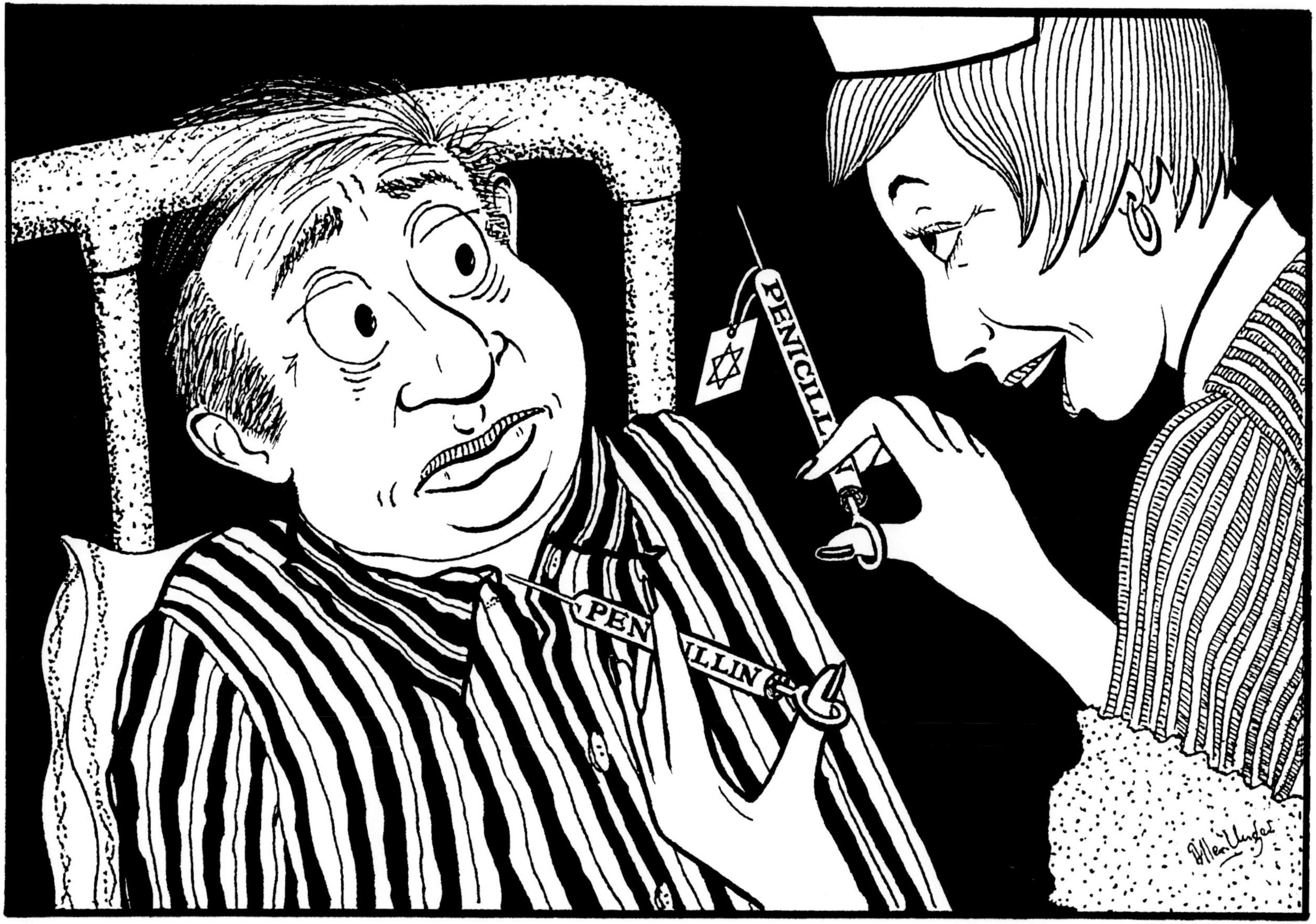
PENICILL
PEN
ILLIN

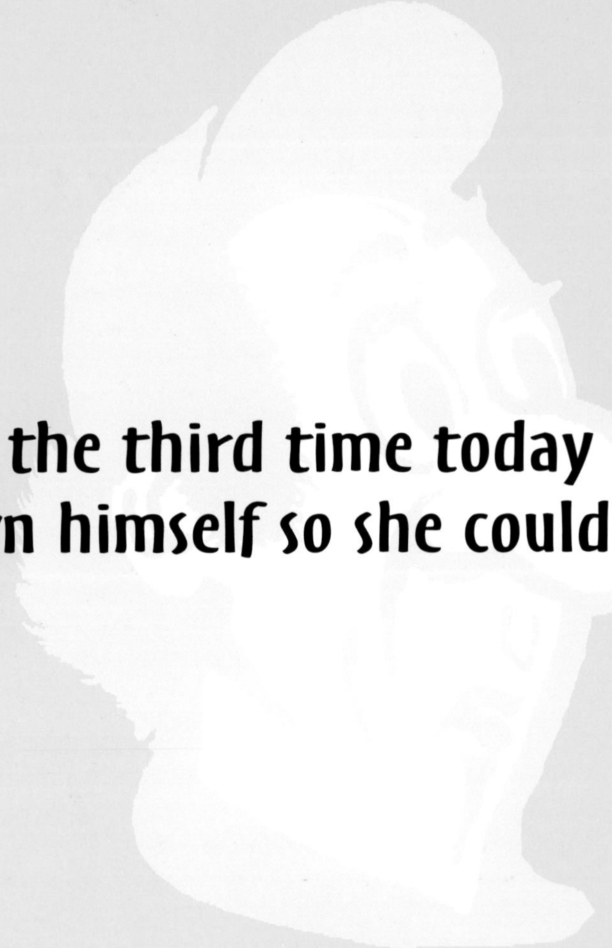

"That's the third time today he's tried to drown himself so she could save him."

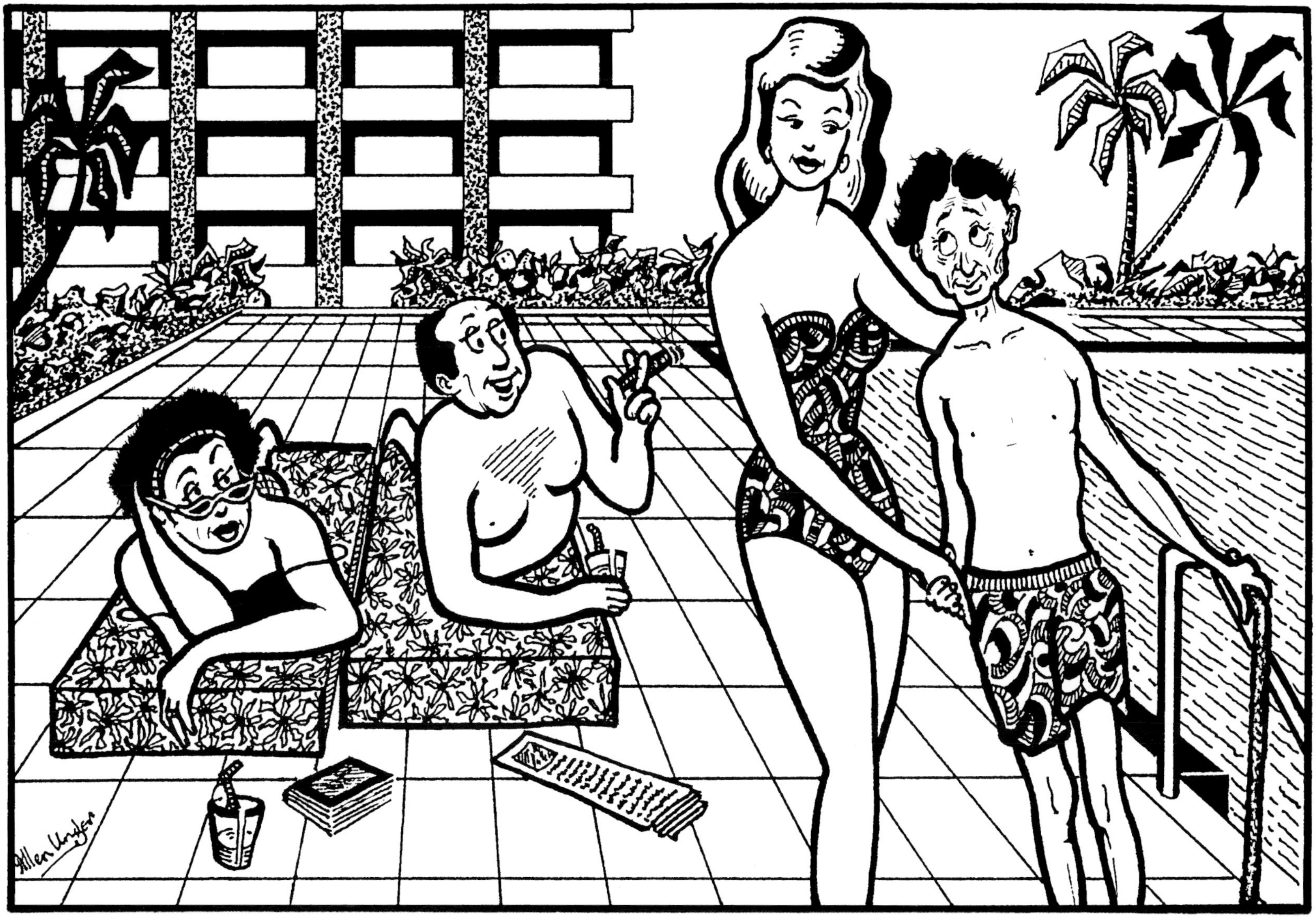
Allen Unger

"Chaim, if this is your way of asking me for a raise, you can forget it."

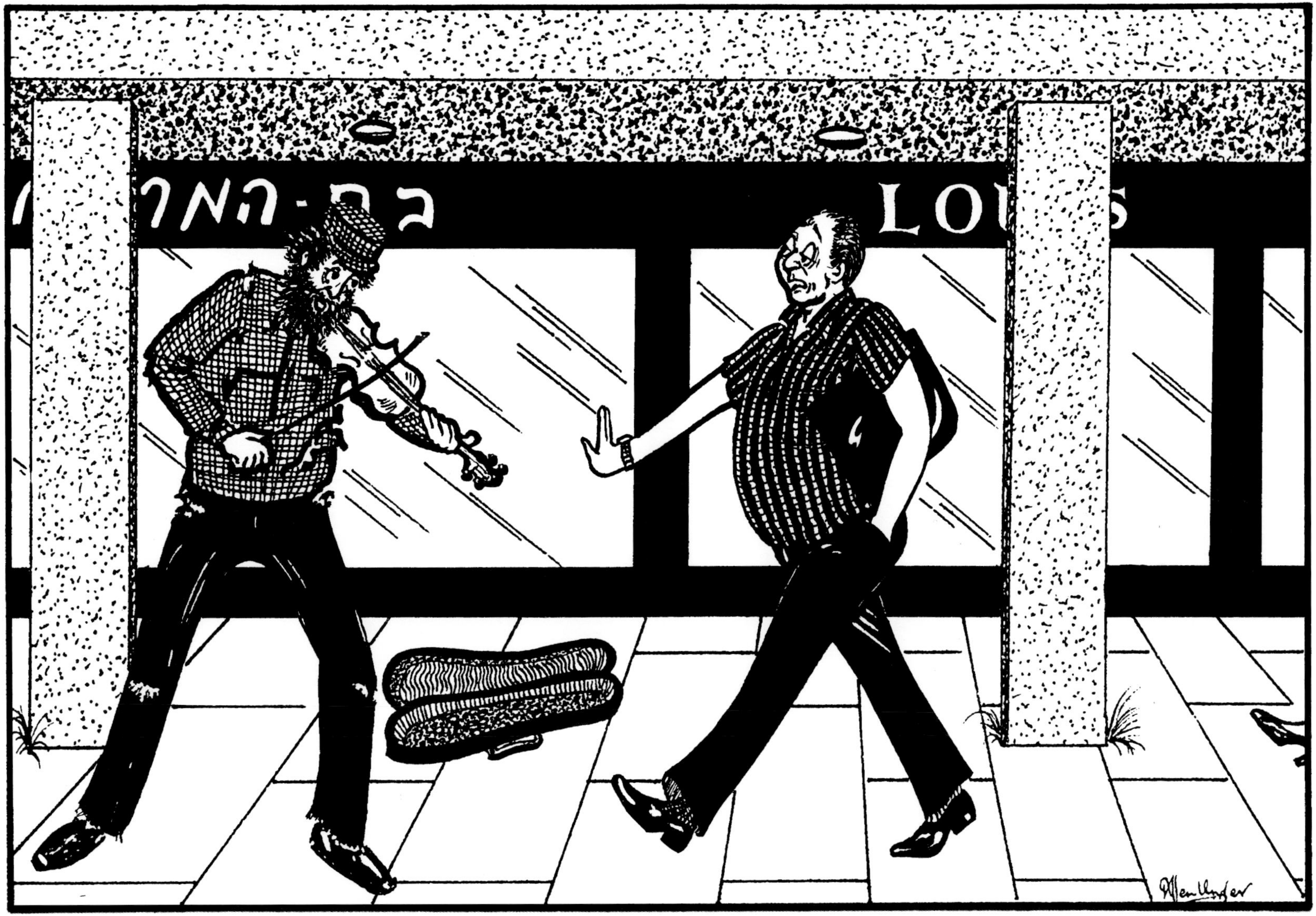

"Regular as clockwork...dashing off after the service, so he can daven mincha... on the golf course."

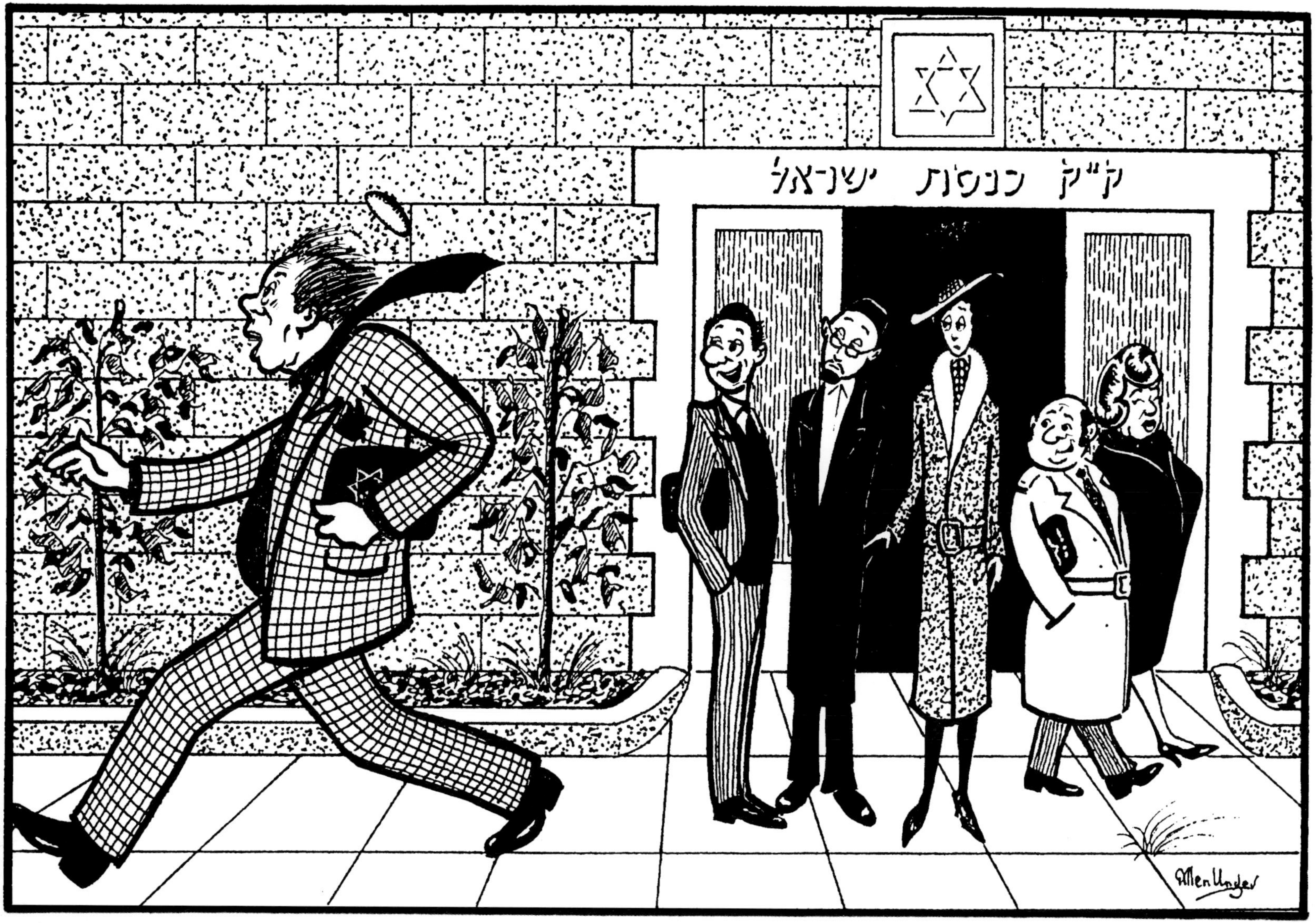
ק״ק כנסת ישראל
AllenUnger

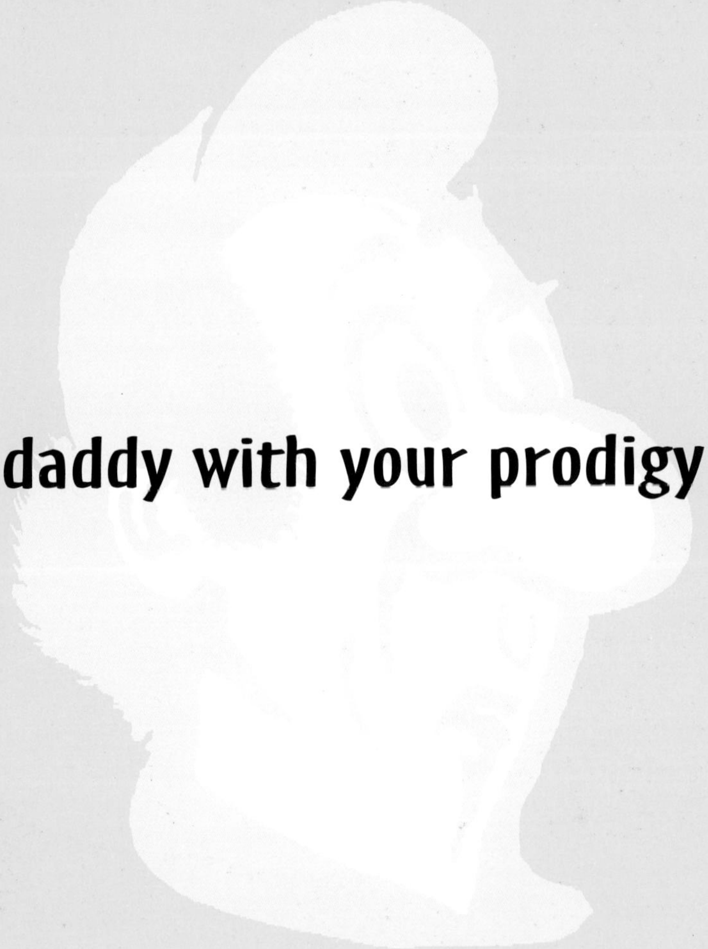

"Here comes daddy with your prodigy playthings!"

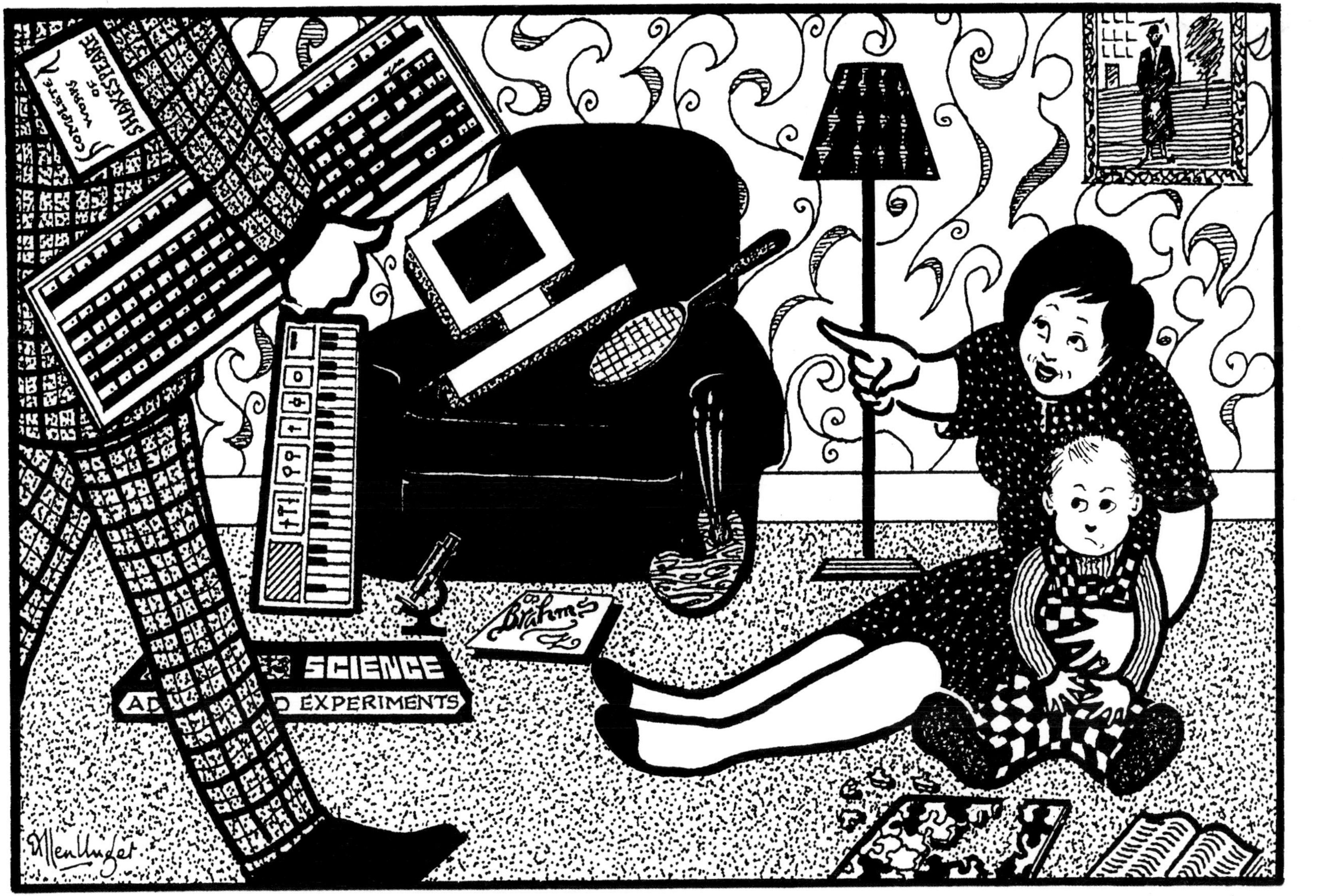
COMPLETE WORKS OF SHAKESPEARE
Brahms
SCIENCE
EXPERIMENTS
Ellen Unger

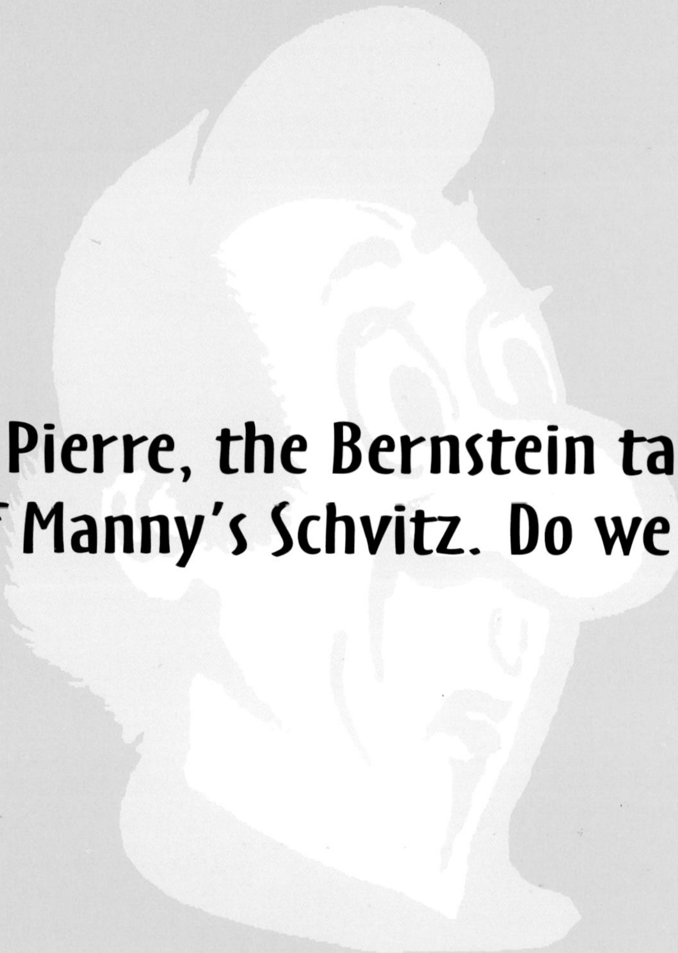

"Ezcusez moi Pierre, the Bernstein table is insisting on a bottle of Manny's Schvitz. Do we know it?"

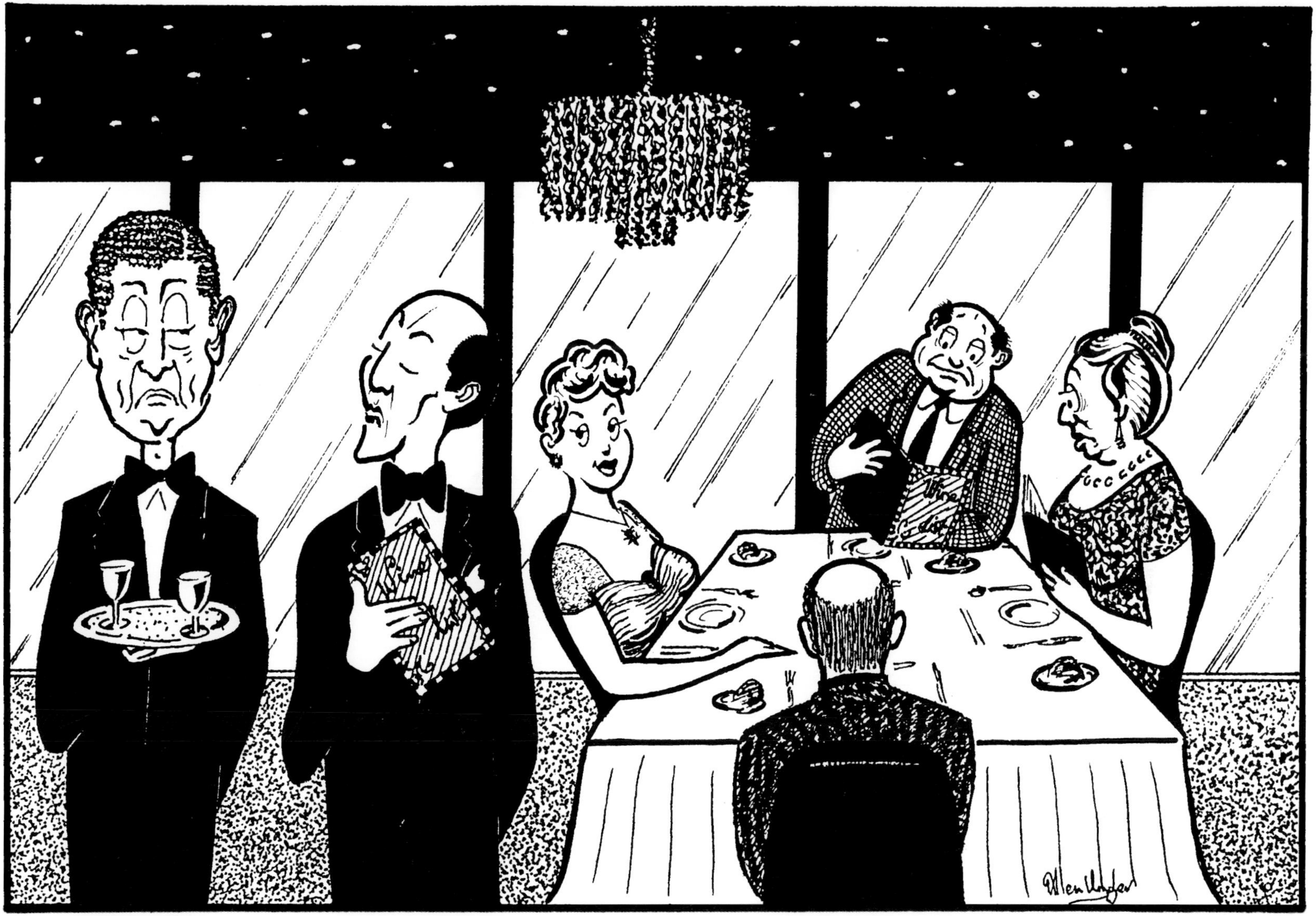

"Alright already...I'll never eat gefilte fish before a performance again..."

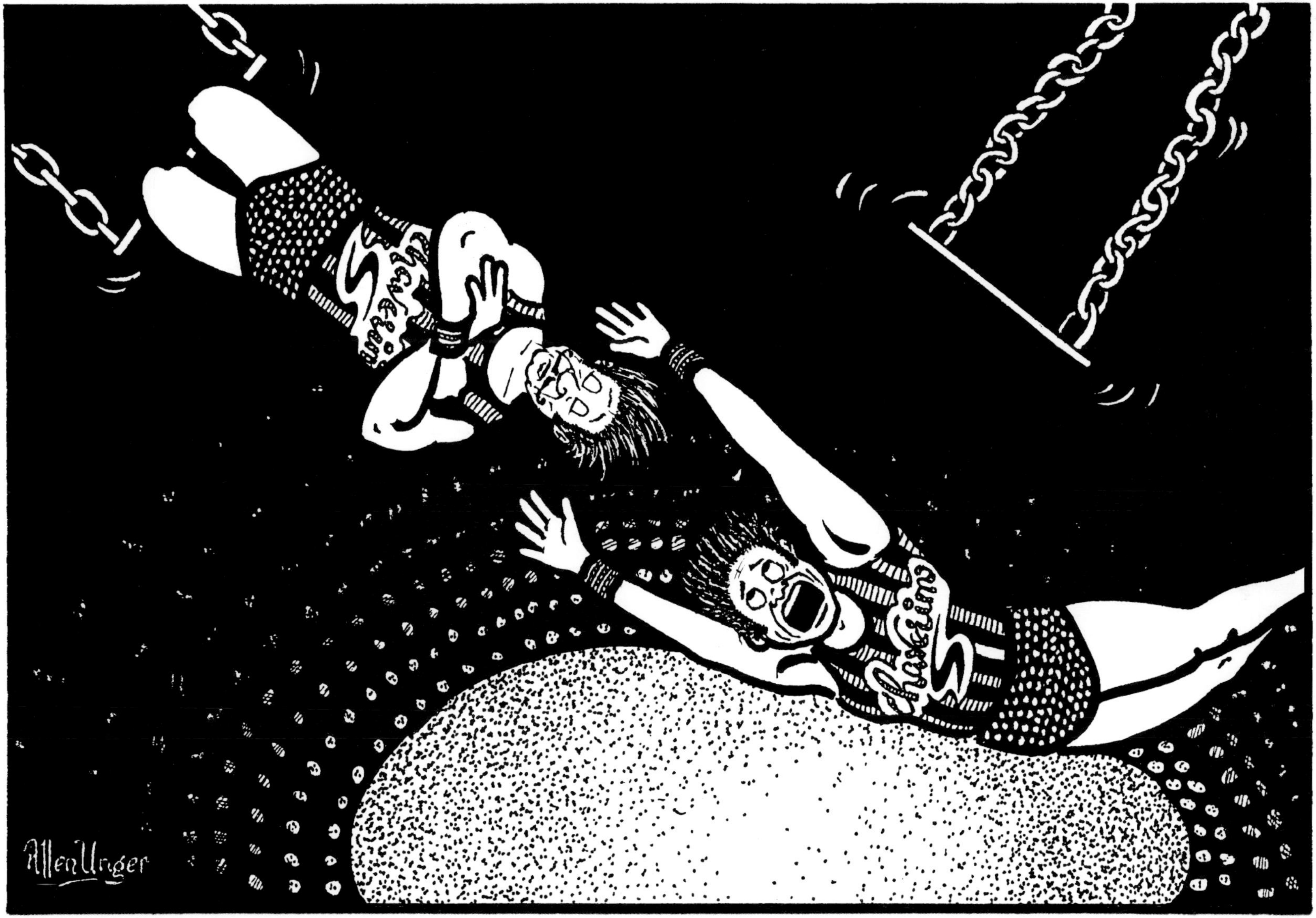
Allen Unger

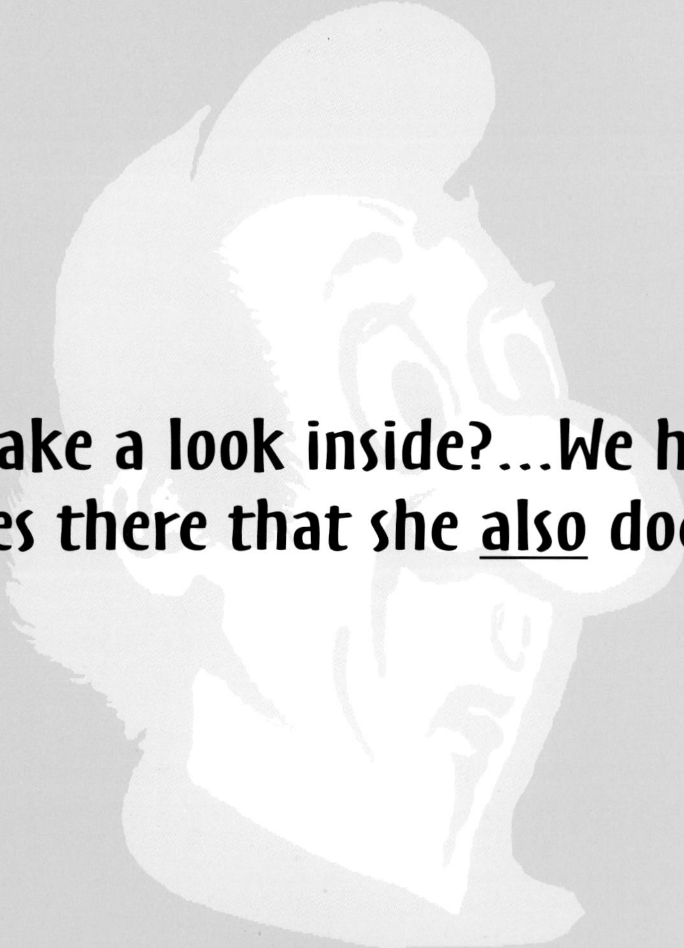

"Why not take a look inside?...We have a lot more dresses there that she also doesn't need."

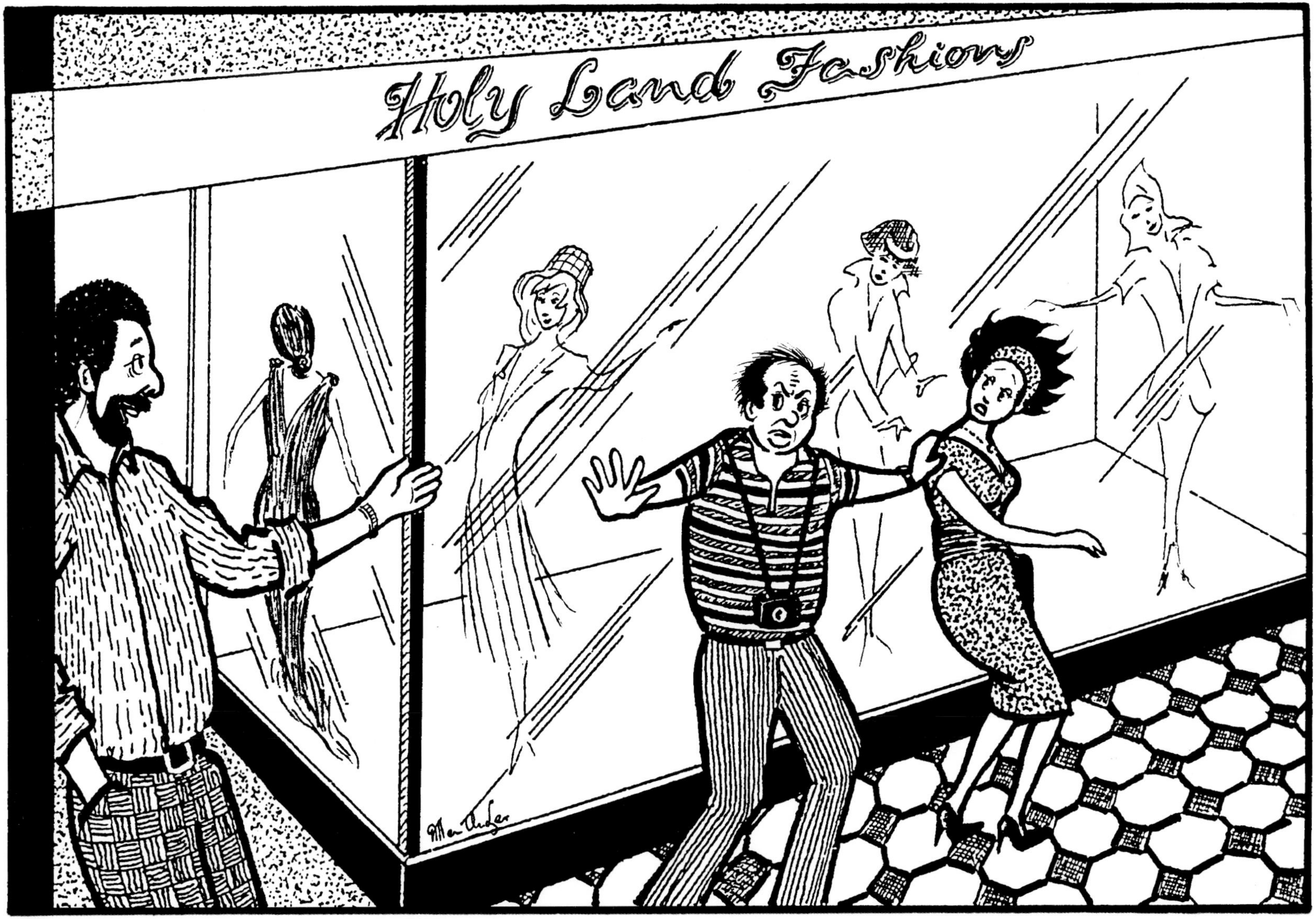
Holy Land Fashions

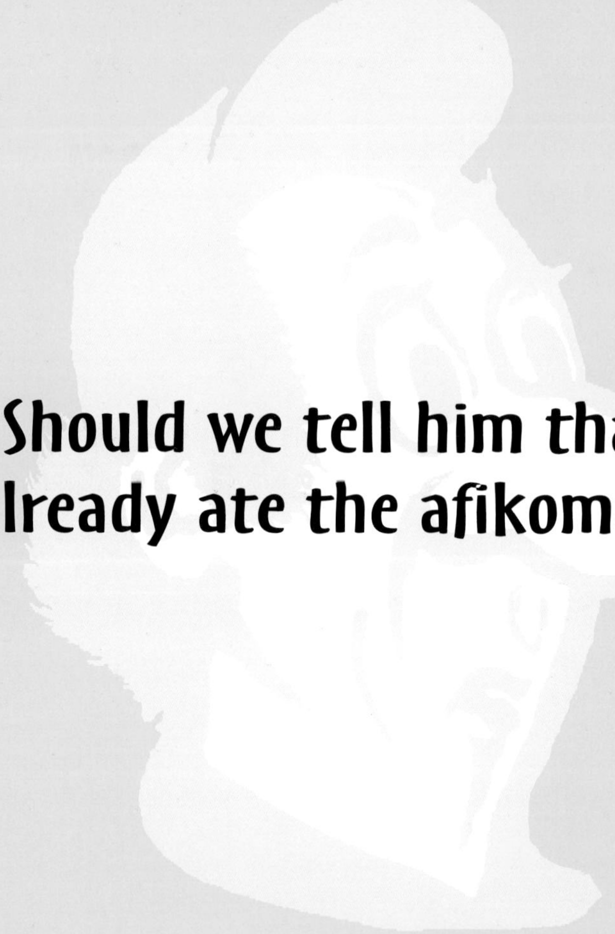

"Should we tell him that we already ate the afikoman?"

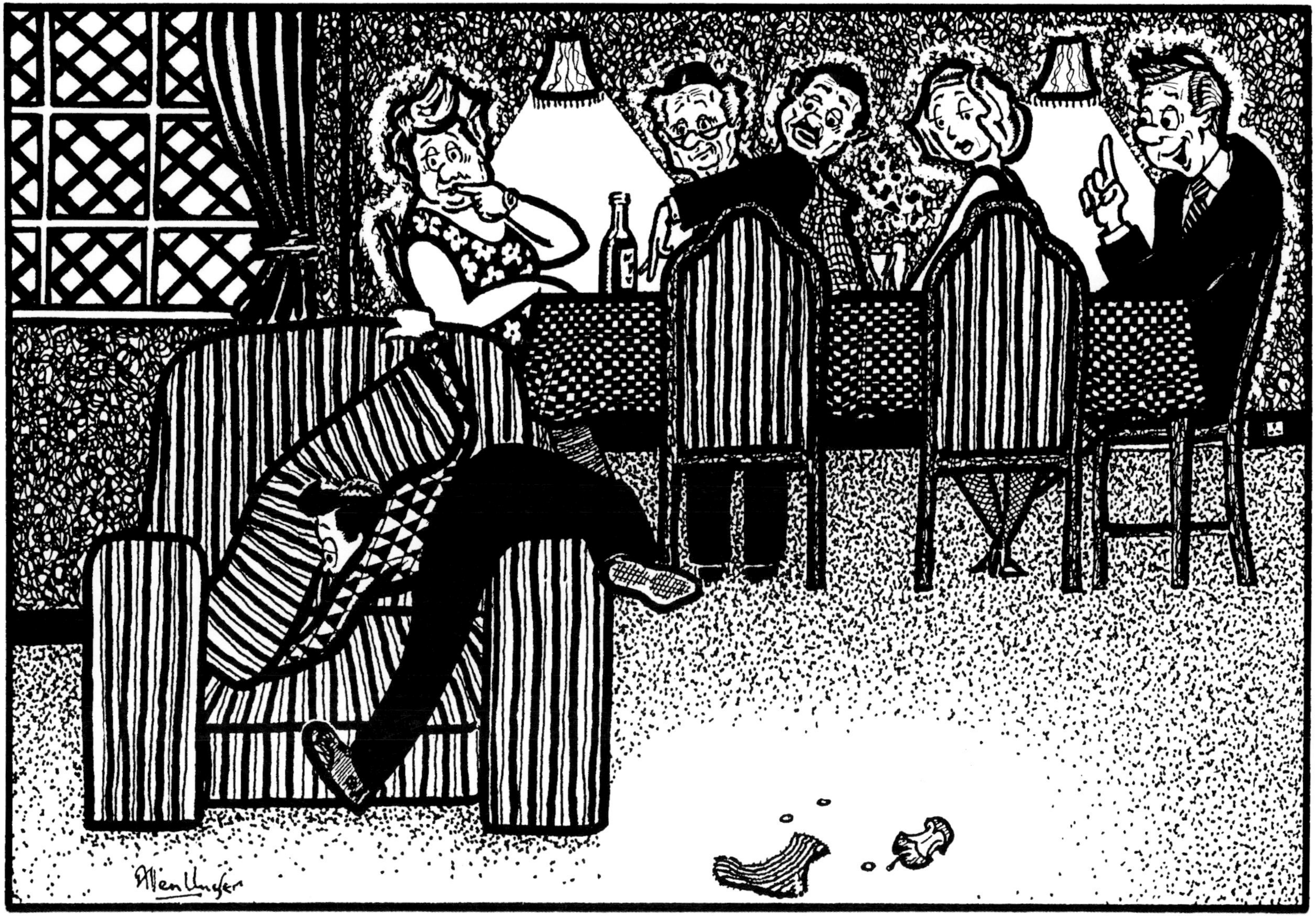
Allen Unger

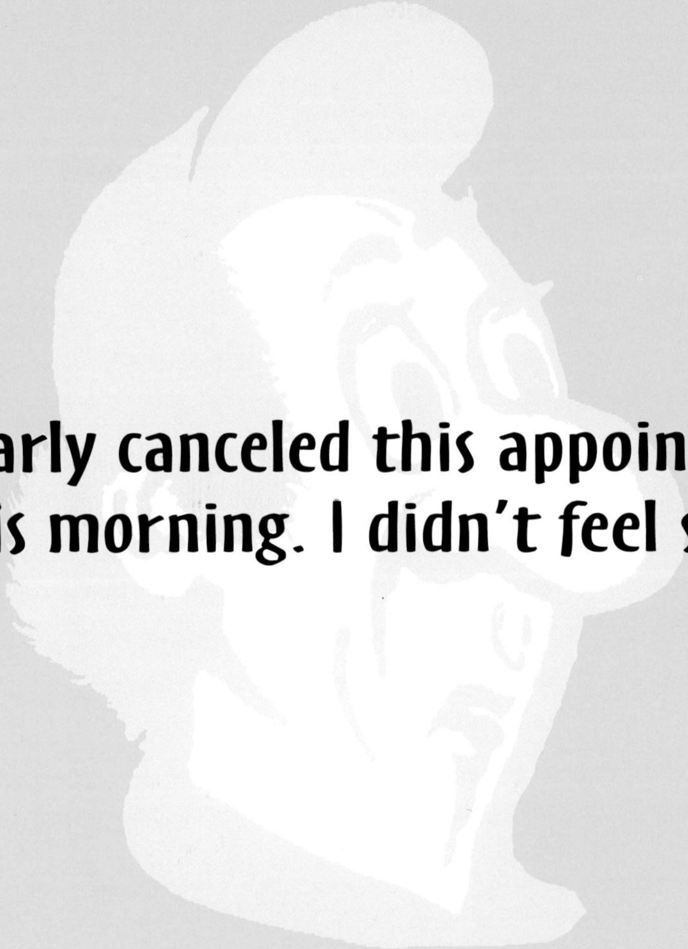

"Doctor, I nearly canceled this appointment when I woke up this morning. I didn't feel so good."

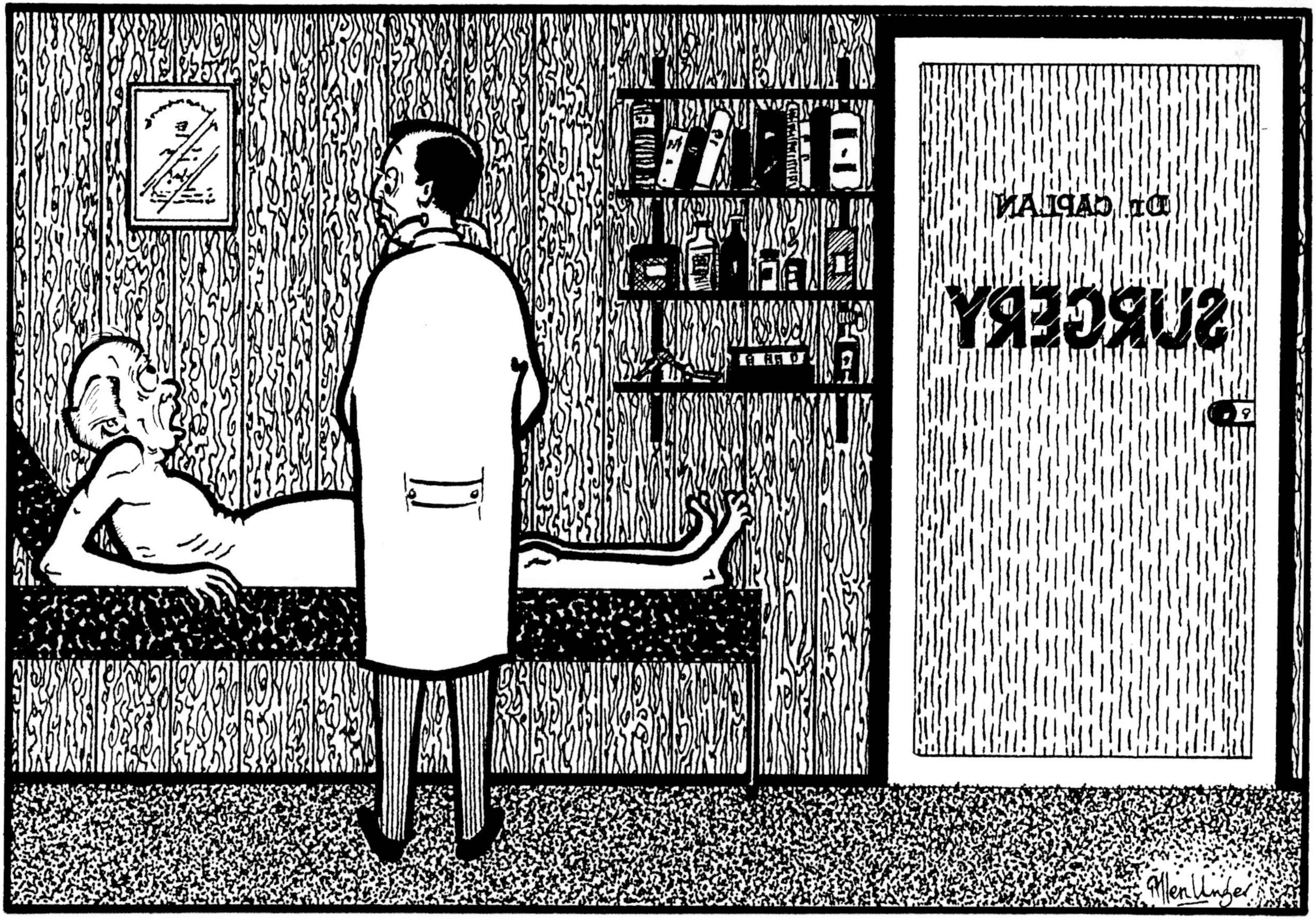
Dr. CAPLAN
SURGERY
Allen Unger

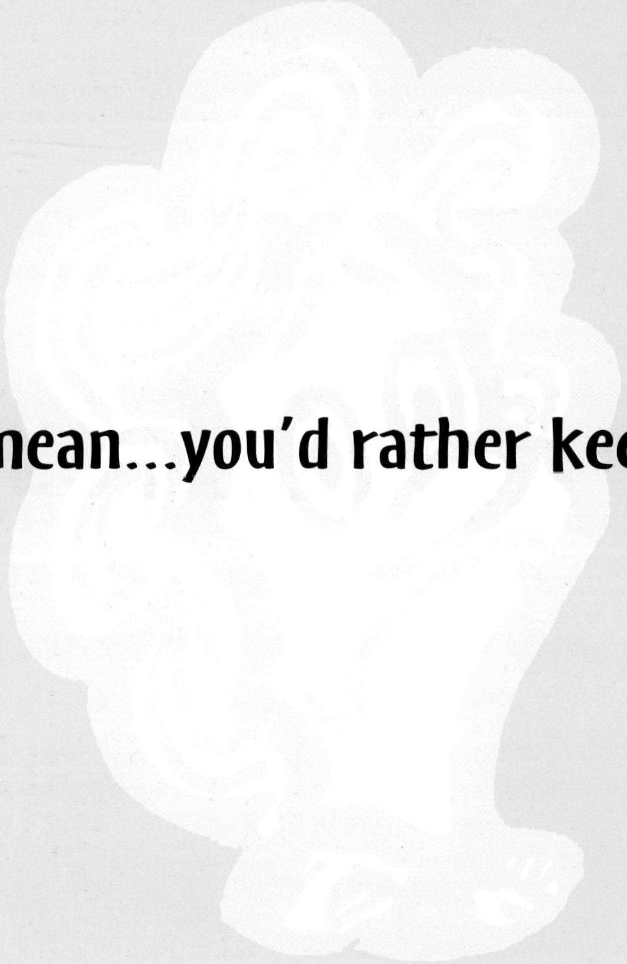

"What do you mean...you'd rather keep the camels?"

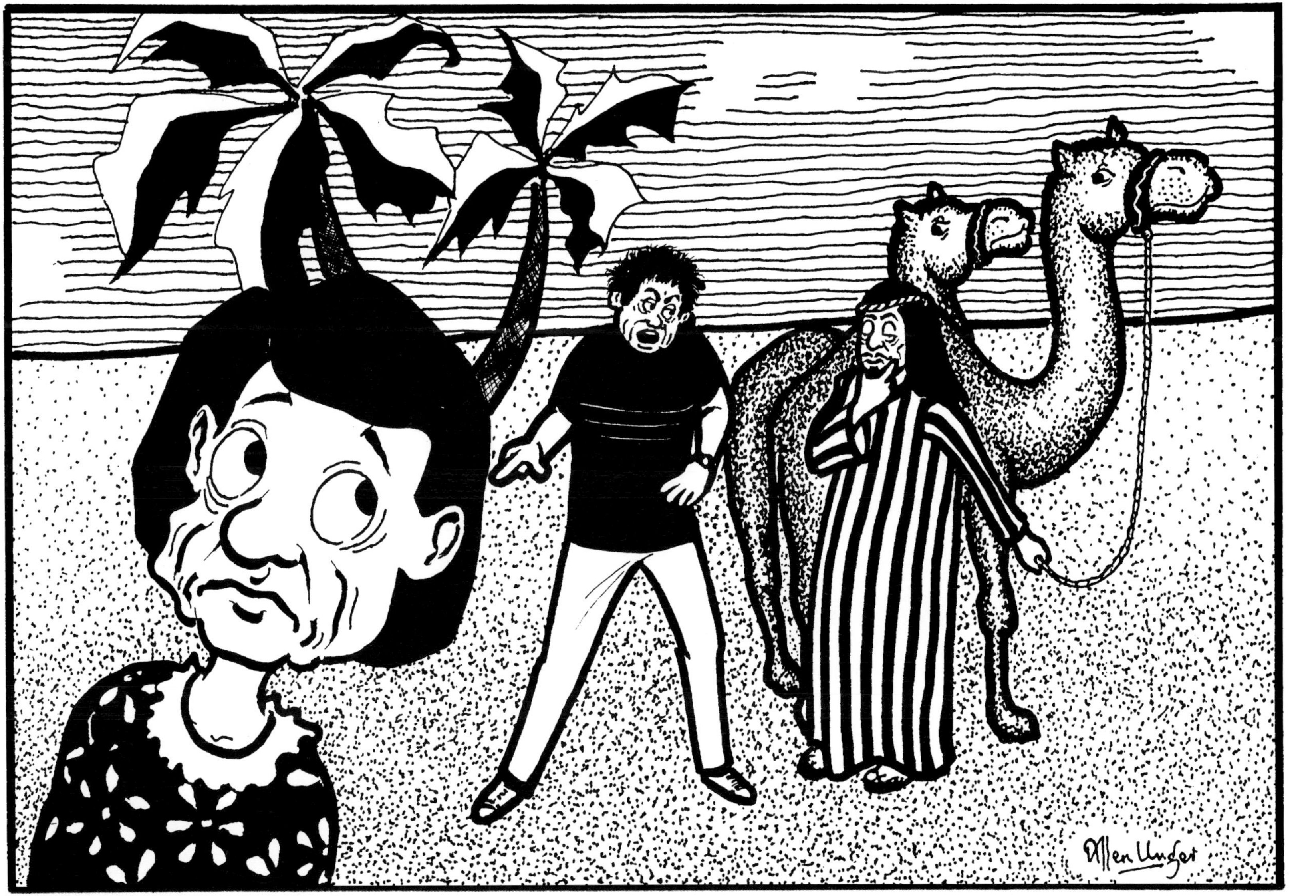
Allen Unger

Glossary

AFIKOMAN	Unleavened bread, hidden during the Passover meal.
BUBBA	Grandmother.
BUBBA-MAYSAH	Tall Story. Old wives tale.
BULVAN	Oaf.
CHOLENT	Type of stew that gently simmers for hours.
FARSCHTUNKANER	Worthless, decrepit.
GEFILTE FISH	Traditional Jewish fish dish.
K'NACKER	A show off. A big shot.
KOSHER	Fit to eat under Jewish Dietary Laws. Honest, genuine.
LUBAVITCH	Ultra-Orthodox Jewish Movement.
MINCHA	Afternoon prayers.
SCHADCHAN	Marriage broker.
SCHLEMIEL	A simple or foolish person.
SCHMATTA	A rag. Cheap junk.
SCHNORRER	A person who collects money for an organization
VERKRIMMT	Seized-up.
UNGESHTOPT	Bloated, over-filled. Obscenely rich.
YEKKE	German or Austrian Jew who is very exacting about time.

Yiddish stubbornly resists translation, so the above is an approximate and affectionate attempt.